Forward Mode

English for Fashion Students

Akie Nyui-Kozuka
Yasue Kawamorita
Kim S. Collins

NAN'UN-DO

Contents

Foreword

For Students

Forward Mode: English for Fashion Students—As the title suggests, this textbook is designed for fashion students. However, this textbook can also be used by non-fashion majors for general English study, as there are a variety of topics that all English learners will enjoy. This book was created with an emphasis on eliciting personal stories that involve students' experiences and emotions. We hope that students will experience the joy of sharing their own stories while using this textbook.

Structure

This textbook consists of 18 units based on various topics. Starting with self-introductions and names, the topics range from family and friends to fashion and the future. It starts with expressing yourself and expands to surrounding people, community, and society. The Appendix also contains vocabulary and activities that will enable you to output specific and detailed fashion-related information. You will learn about fashion-related vocabulary, such as clothes, colors, patterns, materials, trends, and styles from different eras to help you express yourself.

Part 1

On the first page, there is a picture of the author of the Opening Story or the people in the story. Before listening to the Opening Story, please check the Key Words to help you understand the content. The opening stories are all true stories. Enjoy the charm of the personal true stories. The listening questions are not designed to test your comprehension, but rather to ask you what you perceived based on the Opening Story. After the listening questions, there is a transcription of the Opening Story, so if you want to know more about the content, please check it out. Grammar Tips will help you understand the Opening Story well. You can use these grammar tips and they will help you to make your own stories for each topic.

Part 2

We have a set of expression formulas for you to be able to express your own experiences and feelings. You will practice writing English sentences using these patterns.

Part 3

You will practice phrases to facilitate communication; Dialogue will help you understand the function of the target phrase, and Communication Tips will help you identify its function. Practice the target phrases intensively with Try it Out.

Part 4

Students will output what they have learned from Part 1 to 3 in Outcome. Each student will organize their own ideas based on past experiences, feelings, personal preferences, etc. in a step-by-step process before working on the task. Learn and master the brainstorming skills.

Part 5

Reflect on your study using a checklist. By reflecting what you have learned, you will be able to discover what you should learn more about.

Acknowledgments

First and foremost, we would like to thank the wonderful professors of the San Francisco State University MATESOL program. They educated the authors of this book to believe that English education is more than providing learners with linguistic and cultural knowledge and effective communication skills. In fact, they encouraged us to see a new realm of possibilities in our future lives and a way to create a world with more justice and equity. A special thank-you goes to Professor Emeritus H. Douglas Brown and the late Professor Gail Weinstein, who showed us how teachers can welcome a variety of learners of English from different levels and backgrounds, respect diversity, and encourage learners to be the center of the classroom while helping to establish their self-esteem and communication skills. This invaluable experience as learners and also as graduate students has provided us with a solid foundation as English educators and led us to write this English-language textbook for fashion students.

We would also like to extend our appreciation to the members of English Teachers as Agents for Change (ETAC) which consists of SFSU MATESOL graduates. This ETAC study group has made this textbook possible as a collaboration project with the insight, knowledge, and experience of all its members.

Our sincere thanks also goes to Kim S. Collins and Tina M. Ellison, who contributed the illustrations, and weaved their expertise into the field of fashion as fashion designers and English educators in Japan.

We would like to acknowledge the valuable contribution from the students at Sugino Fashion College and Dressmaker Gakuin in Tokyo who were the motivation for creating this textbook; they contributed to our recursive process of designing teaching materials for more than 10 years. We especially thank Saki, Karia, and Kyoko who provided true stories to our Opening Stories Unit 1, 2, and 3.

We would like to acknowledge each storyteller for the Opening Story: Saki (Unit 1), Kyoko (Unit 2), Karia (Unit 3), Padi (Unit 5), Roozbeh (Unit 10), Tracy (Unit 13), and Chiaki (Unit 18).

The authors would like to thank the publication team at NAN'UN-DO, especially Atsushi Kato and Takumi Fukuzaki.

Lastly, we thank the families of the authors. Besides our daily work and responsibilities both at home and at work as English educators, we spent an enormous amount of time on this textbook project early in the mornings, in the evenings, and on weekends. Without your support and collaboration, we could not have come to achieve this goal.

Editors and Writers
October 2022

Download Audio

音声ファイル
無料 DL
のご案内

このテキストの音声を無料で視聴（ストリーミング）・ダウンロードできます。自習用音声としてご活用ください。
以下のサイトにアクセスしてテキスト番号で検索してください。

https://nanun-do.com テキスト番号［**512185**］

※ 無線 LAN（WiFi）に接続してのご利用を推奨いたします。

※ 音声ダウンロードは Zip ファイルでの提供になります。
お使いの機器によっては別途ソフトウェア（アプリケーション）の導入が必要となります。

Forward Mode 音声ダウンロードページは
左記の QR コードからもご利用になれます。

Unit 1
MY NAME STORY

Part 1 Exploring the Topic

1-1 First Impression

I Love
My Name

Profile

Saki was born and raised in Tokyo, Japan. She is studying fashion business and creation at Dressmaker Gakuin in Tokyo. She enjoys designing and making costumes.

Look at the picture and the title. Write your predictions about the story.
写真とタイトルを見てみましょう。ストーリーについて、あなたの予想を書きましょう。

1-2 Listening

02

Key Words

kanji character 漢字　mean (v) 意味する　bloom 花が咲く、開花する、輝く
pronounce 発音する　first name/given name 名前　grow 成長する
syllable 音節、一音　add 加える　bond 繋がり、絆

Listen to the Opening Story and answer the following questions.
オープニングストーリーを聴いて、以下の質問について答えましょう。

1. What is the author's name? How does she feel about her name?
2. Do you know who gave you your name?
3. Do you like your family/first/middle name? Why? Why not?

1-3 Opening Story

Read and check the contents of the Opening Story you heard in the Listening Section.
リスニングで聴いた Opening Story の内容を確認しましょう。

I Love My Name

My name is Saki. My parents named me. What is in my name? The kanji character for "Sa" means to bloom and "ki" means the moon. "Saki" means a blooming moon or the moon blooms. Many people pronounce my name "Satsuki" when they see the *kanji* characters, but it is pronounced "Saki." When I was born, my parents saw the beautiful moon in the sky and imagined it would be blooming in the dark night. Then they gave me this first name.

My parents wanted each of their daughters to grow and bloom like flowers in their lives. I have two older sisters, Hazuki and Natsuki. Combining the first parts of our names gives us "Ha Na Saku." This means "a flower in bloom" in Japanese. I feel a special bond among the three of us. I love my given name.

1-4 Grammar Tips

It is important to ask questions to show you are interested in the person you are talking to. You can ask specific questions with WH questions: what, who, where, when, why and how.

質問をして､会話の相手に対して興味を示すことは大切です。WH から始まる疑問詞を使って､What(何)､Who(誰)､Where(どこ)、When（いつ)、Why（なぜ)、How（どうやって）とより具体的に質問できます。

WH-Question What	**Be Verb** is	**Subject** your nickname?		
WH-Question Why	**do/does/did** do	**Subject** you	**Verb** like	**Object** it?
WH-Question Who	**Action verb** named			**Object** you?

Part 2 Expressing Yourself

A. Practice writing about yourself in English using some of the expressions below. Use the examples in the parentheses as a reference and change the colored parts into your own words.

下記の表現の型を使って、自分のことを書けるようにしましょう。括弧内の例を参考にして茶色の部分を自分の言葉に置き換えてください。

名前の意味 : What does your name mean?

1. My name is <**Saki**>. “**Sa**” means to bloom and “**ki**” means **the moon**.
   (your name) (meanings of the character)

名付けた人 : Who named you?

2. **My parents** named me. (e.g., a monk, a naming specialist)
3. I was named by **my brother**. (e.g., grandfather, uncle)

名付けの理由 : Why did your parent(s) choose your name?

4. My parent wanted me to become a **gentle** person. (e.g., famous, smart)
5. My parents wanted to use ***hiragana*** for each name of their children.
   (e.g., the same *kanji* character, the letter K)

6. I was given one *kanji* character from each of my parents' name. I got "<**Ma**>" from my father, <**Masato**> and "<**Yu**>" from my mother, <**Yumiko**>.
7. My mother liked **the sound** of the name. (e.g., *kanji* character, origin)
8. My father chose a middle name that goes well with my **given name**. (e.g., our surname, our family name)
9. I was named after **my grandfather**. (e.g., a popular singer, a famous athlete)

B. Write about your name in English using the sentences/phrases/expressions above.
上記の文章 / 句 / 表現を参考に自分の名前について英語で文章を作りましょう。

Meaning of your name (if any): ______________________________
Who gave you your name? ______________________________
Why was the name chosen? ______________________________

Part 3 Communication Practice

3-1 Dialogue: Asking Questions

Please take a look at Example 1 and 2. Which conversation is better? Why?
下記の 2 つの対話を見てみましょう。どちらの例が良い対話ですか。なぜでしょうか。

Example 1

Jim: Hi, I am Jim. Nice to meet you.

Akie: Hi, I am Akie. Nice to meet you too.

Jim: Oh, that's a nice name.

Akie: Thank you.

Jim: Yes. ....

Example 2

Jim: Hi, I am Jim. Nice to meet you.

Akie: Hi, I am Akie. Nice to meet you too.

Jim: Oh, that's a nice name. "Aki" means fall, right? And "e" means blessing.

Akie: Oh, no. Actually, my name has a different *kanji*.

Jim: What does your name mean?

Akie: It means a picture of a rising sun.

Jim: I see. That's beautiful.

Akie: Thank you. How about you?

3-2 Communication Tips: Asking Questions

Asking questions keeps a conversation going and you can also find something you have in common. It is sociable and gives a good impression.
質問することで会話は弾み、共通点を見つけることもできます。社交的で、良い印象を与えることができます。

3-3 Try It Out

Question Words (WH-Questions)

誰	何	どこ	いつ	なぜ	どのように	いくつ
Who ...?	**What ...?**	**Where ...?**	**When ...?**	**Why ...?**	**How ...?**	**How many ...?**

Practice using the above expressions of "Question Words."
上記の「疑問詞」を使って質問する練習をしましょう。

Student A: Choose a topic from the box below, and say "Please ask me about (the topic you chose)."
下記の四角の中からトピックを選び、"Please ask me about (選んだトピック)" で会話を始めます。

Student B: Ask as many questions on the topic as possible.
そのトピックに関して、WH 疑問文を使ってできるだけ多く質問しましょう。

Switch the roles of A and B when finished.
その後、A と B の役割を交代しましょう。

Example

Student A: Please ask me about "**nicknames**."

Student B: Yes, sure. What is your nickname?

Student A: My nickname is Akipon. And I have some more nicknames.

Student B: How many nicknames do you have?

Student A: I have five nicknames.

Student B: What are they?

Topics

1. nicknames **2. first name** **3. pets** **4. hometown** **5. your idea**

Part 4 Outcome

Follow the steps below. Then introduce the story of your name. Present it with pictures or illustrations.

以下のステップに従ってください。そして、自分の名前のストーリーを紹介します。写真やイラストを使いながら、以下の手順で紹介してください。

Step 1: Brainstorming: Think of anything you know about your name by using a mind map for brainstorming ideas and information. Start with the main topic and add sub topics. Then write down any examples that are connected to the sub topics.

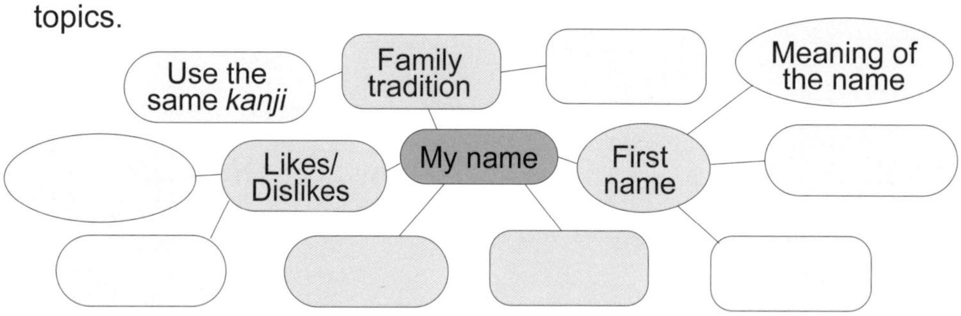

Example: Create a mind map about your name.

Preparation: Discuss the questions with your partner.

1. Do you like your name? Why? Why not?
2. What are your family's naming traditions?

Step 2: Organizing your ideas: Decide what and how you tell the story of your name.

Step 3: Telling your story: Tell your story to your partner.

Step 4: Creating visuals: Make a collage based on your story and explain it to your classmates.

Part 5 Reflection

Check your progress. Circle the numbers below.

今回のレッスンを振り返りましょう。下の番号に○を付けましょう。

Now I can ...	← ---- →
1. talk about the topic of this unit. (my name)	1---2---3---4---5
2. write about myself using the expressions in Part 2.	1---2---3---4---5
3. use the communication tips in Part 3. (asking questions: WH-questions)	1---2---3---4---5
4. talk about my personal experience/feelings. (my name)	1---2---3---4---5

Unit 2 DESCRIBING MYSELF

Part 1 Exploring the Topic

1-1 First Impression

Different, Therefore Strong

Profile

Kyoko graduated from Sugino Fashion College in Tokyo and has been working as a fashion designer for 6 years at an apparel company. She started her apparel company HIKARI underwear with her best friend from college.

Look at the picture and the title. Write your predictions about the story.

写真とタイトルを見てみましょう。ストーリーについて、あなたの予想を書きましょう。

1-2 Listening

03

Key Words

worries 心配事、悩み事　anxiety 不安　underwear 下着　convey 伝える
accept 受け入れる　cautious 慎重な　critically analyze 批判的に分析する
carefully observant 注意深い　function (v) 機能する
empowerment エンパワメント、力付けること

Listen to the Opening Story and answer the following questions.
オープニングストーリーを聴いて、以下の質問について答えましょう。

1. What is Kyoko's occupation? What does she often worry about?
2. How does Hitomi support Kyoko so that she can step forward?
3. Do you have someone who can help you when you need it?

1-3 Opening Story

Read and check the contents of the Opening Story you heard in the Listening Section.
リスニングで聴いた Opening Story の内容を確認しましょう。

Different, Therefore Strong

I enjoy my work as a fashion designer in Tokyo. However, I sometimes have worries and anxiety. When I was 27 years old, I started up an underwear design company, HIKARI underwear, with my best friend, Hitomi. I often worry if I can convey what I want to express in the products or if my designs can be accepted by others. I feel like disappearing while creating new designs, and feel lost and nervous. It is like wandering in a dark tunnel without an exit.

However, Hitomi, the art director and business manager, is opposite to me. She is always energetic and forward thinking. She is open-minded and accepts what I create. Not only just accepting my ideas, she critically analyzes my designs and products in a positive manner. She also creates space for me to be free and creative, so that I can step forward with positive energy. On the contrary, Hitomi says she can trust me because I tend to be cautious and carefully observant.

As a team, we have been functioning very well together. We have different personalities, but with trust, respect, and empowerment, we can move forward more powerfully together.

1-4 Grammar Tips

When referring to a person, in order to avoid repeating proper names, you use personal pronouns. The third person singular of the personal pronouns used to be he, she, and it, but in recent years, the third person singular to express nonbinary Singular *they* has come into use. As with the third person plural they, the verb takes the plural form. Think of the ways verbs are used for singular and plural "you." For a more detailed description of Singular *they*, see Appendix 1.

人物に言及する時、固有名詞を繰り返すことを避けて、人称代名詞を使います。人称代名詞の3人称単数は he, she, it の3種が使われてきましたが、近年ではノンバイナリーを表す3人称単数の Singular *they* も使用されるようになってきました。これは、3人称複数の they と同様に動詞は複数形を取ります。単数と複数の you の場合と同様に考えましょう。Singular *they* に関するより詳しい説明は Appendix 1 を参照してください。

Example

Hikaru is my best friend. **They** are very cheerful and I like **their** personality.

Part 2 Expressing Yourself

A. Practice writing about yourself in English using some of the expressions below. Use the examples in the parentheses as a reference and change the colored parts into your own words.

下記の表現の型を使って、自分のことを書けるようにしましょう。括弧内の例を参考にして茶色の部分の単語を自分の言葉に置き換えてください。

あなたの性格についての表現：What is your character?

1. I am **hardworking**. (e.g., organized, optimistic, patient)

2. I think I am a **generous** person. (e.g., messy, pessimistic, jealous)

あなたがそう思う理由：Why do you think so?

3. I'm **hardworking** because I **have three different part-time jobs**, and study hard.
(e.g., studious, responsible, competitive)
(e.g., clean my room everyday, take notes on everything)

4. I'm **quiet**. I **cannot talk much with new people**.
(e.g., outgoing, shy) (e.g., like to meet new people, cannot make good eye contact)

あなたの大切な人についての表現：Who do you usually talk to?

5. I talk about everything to my best friend, <**Tomo**>.
   He is a very **helpful** person.
   (e.g., She is, They are) (e.g., optimistic, considerate)

6. My **friend** is like my **brother**.
   (e.g., brother, cousin) (e.g., counselor, sister)
   She is a good listener and we get along well.
   (e.g., He is, They are) (e.g., a funny person, an energetic person)

B. Write about your character and the reason in English using the sentences/phrases/expressions above.
上記の文章 / 句 / 表現を参考に自分の性格とそう思う理由について英語で文章を作りましょう。

Your character: ______________________________

Reasons: ______________________________

Part 3 Communication Practice

3-1 Dialogue: Asking Questions (Yes/No Questions)

Please take a look at Example 1 and 2. Which conversation is better? Why?
下記の 2 つの対話を見てみましょう。どちらの例が良い対話ですか。なぜでしょうか。

Example 1

Yasue: What do you like to do in your free time?

Sam: Umm. I like watching movies.

Yasue: What is your favorite movie?

Sam: I cannot choose one... Ummmm....“*The Lord of the Rings.*”

Yasue: Why do you like it?

Sam: Ummm....

Example 2

Yasue: Do you have a lot of free time on weekends?

Sam: Yes, I do.

Yasue: What do you usually do?

Sam: I watch movies.

Yasue: Have you watched “*The Lord of the Rings*”?

Sam: Yes. It is a great movie.

Yasue: It is. Do you like it too?

Sam: Yes. I like the characters’ personalities and the story.

3-2 Communication Tips: Asking Questions (Yes/No Questions)

In Unit 1, you learned about WH-Questions. Another form of question is the Yes/No Question. It is relatively easier to answer than the WH-Question because the person being asked only has to answer "yes" or "no."

Unit 1 では、WH-Questions について学びました。もう一つの疑問文の形は Yes/No Question です。質問される側には答え方が２つの選択肢しかないので、WH- Questions よりも比較的簡単に答えることができます。

3-3 Try It Out

Yes/No Questions

一般動詞の文の場合	助動詞が含まれる文の場合	be 動詞の文の場合	現在完了形の文の場合
Do ...? **Does ...?**	**Can ...?** **Will ...?**	**Are you ...?** **Is it ...?**	**Have you ...?** **Has it ...?**

Practice using the above expressions of "Yes/No Questions."
Yes/No Questions を使って質問する練習をしましょう。

Student A: Choose a topic from the box below and say to Student B, "Please ask me about (the topic you chose)."
下記の四角の中からトピックを選び、"Please ask me about (選んだトピック)." と言います。

Student B: Ask as many questions on the topic as possible. Please start with a Yes/No question.
そのトピックに関して、疑問文を使ってできるだけ多く質問しましょう。Yes/No Question から始めましょう。

Switch the roles of A and B when finished.
その後、A と B の役割を交代しましょう。

Example

Student A: Please ask me about "**friends**."

Student B: Yes, sure. Do you have any good friends at school?

Student A: Yes, I do.

Student B: Did you meet them in class?

Student A: No, I met them at the art club.

Student B: What do you usually do with them?

Topics

1. friends　**2. family**　**3. favorite things**　**4. your personality**　**5. your idea**

Part 4 Outcome

Follow the steps below. Then introduce the story of your character and/or the character of family/ friends. Present it with pictures or illustrations.

以下のステップに従ってください。そして、自分の性格やそれに関連した家族・友達の性格についてのストーリーを紹介します。写真やイラストを使いながら、以下の手順で紹介してください。

Step 1: Brainstorming: Think of what you want to say about your own chracter and characters of your family and friends related to it. You can write a list to organize your ideas.

Example:

My Character

-
-
-

Step 2: Organizing your ideas: Decide what information from your list to keep and what information to leave out.

Step 3: Adding details: Add more information about your character and/or the character of family/friends.

Step 4: Telling your story: Tell your story to your partner.

Step 5: Creating visuals: Make a collage based on your story and explain it.

Part 5 Reflection

Check your progress. Circle the numbers below.

今回のレッスンを振り返りましょう。下の番号に○を付けましょう。

Now I can ...	← ---- →
1. talk about the topic of this unit. (describing myself)	1---2---3---4---5
2. write about myself using the expressions in Part 2.	1---2---3---4---5
3. use the communication tips in Part 3. (asking questions: Yes/No Questions)	1---2---3---4---5
4. talk about my personal experience/feelings. (my character)	1---2---3---4---5

Unit 3 FRIENDS AND FAMILY IN MY HOMETOWN

Part 1 Exploring the Topic

1-1 First Impression

What I Miss the Most

Profile

Karia was born and raised in Mexico. She lives in Tokyo studying fashion business and creation at Dress Maker Gakuin, a vocational school for fashion.

Look at the picture and the title. Write your predictions about the story.
写真とタイトルを見てみましょう。ストーリーについて、あなたの予想を書きましょう。

1-2 Listening

04

Key Words

Durango [du'raŋgo] メキシコの北西部の州の町　being away from ~　~から離れて
greet　挨拶する　cheek　頬　emotion　感情　physical contact　肌の触れ合い
after graduating　卒業後　interactions　やりとり、交流

Listen to the Opening Story and answer the following questions.
オープニングストーリーを聴いて、以下の質問について答えましょう。

1. Where is Karia from?
2. What do you like about your hometown?
3. Do you want to go back to/stay in your hometown?

1-3 Opening Story

Read and check the contents of the Opening Story you heard in the Listening Section.
リスニングで聴いた Opening Story の内容を確認しましょう。

What I Miss the Most

I am from a small town, Durango in Mexico, but I live in Tokyo now and study fashion. This is my first time being away from my hometown for more than three months. I sometimes miss my family, friends, and the little things of everyday life in my hometown. One of them is how people greet and communicate with each other. People in my hometown kiss each other on the cheek, hug and smile a lot. Although I don't do much of these things, I really like to see people showing their full emotions.

Now I'm in Tokyo. People in Tokyo seem to have much less physical contact with family and friends compared to what I've experienced in Durango. Many people are polite and show respect by bowing. It is true that I cannot wait to see my family and friends after graduating, but I also enjoy being with different people who interact in different ways.

1-4 Grammar Tips

The subject and the verb are important elements of an English sentence. If even one of them is missing, the meaning of the sentence is lost, and the missing sentence is called <Fragments>.

主語と動詞は英語の文を構成するための大事な要素です。一つでも抜けると意味が通じなくなります。重要な構成要素が抜けた文を＜ Fragments ＞と呼びます。

Correct: **I am from** Durango in Mexico, but I live in Tokyo now and study fashion.

Wrong: **I from** Durango in Mexico, but I live in Tokyo now and study fashion.

Part 2 Expressing Yourself

A. Practice writing about yourself in English using some of the expressions below. Use the examples in the parentheses as a reference and change the colored parts into your own words.

下記の表現の型を使って、自分のことを書けるようにしましょう。括弧内の例を参考にして茶色の部分の単語を自分の言葉に置き換えてください。

出身地ついて話す表現：Where are you from?

1. I am from **Durango in Mexico**.
   (town or city you are from)

2. I was born and raised in **a small town** in Japan.
   (e.g., a big city, a port town, an island, a mountain village)

故郷の好きなところについて話す表現：What do you like about your hometown?

3. I sometimes miss **my family, friends, and just the little things**.
   (e.g., my friends from high school, my dog, local food)

4. Now I'm in **Tokyo** and realize that people in my hometown
   (where you live now)
   have much physical contact with family and friends.
   (e.g., are more traditional, are kind)

今住んでいる場所について話す表現：Where do you live?

5. I live in **Hachinohe**. It is **in northern Japan**.
   (e.g., north of Tokyo, Fukushima, Kobe) (e.g., south of Japan, northeast of Japan)

6. I **like** where I live now because **there are opportunities to meet interesting people**.
(e.g., don't like, love) (e.g., it doesn't have a good vibe, there are many beautiful parks)

人々について話す表現 : What are they like?

7. People in my hometown seem mostly **liberal**.
(e.g., conservative, laidback, helpful)

B. Write about your hometown and give the reasons in English using the sentences/phrases/expressions above.
上記の文章 / 句 / 表現を参考に自分の故郷 / 地元やそこに住む人たちについて英語で文章を作りましょう。

Your hometown neighborhood: ______________________________

____

People from your hometown: ______________________________

____

Part 3 Communication Practice

3-1 Dialogue: Showing Reactions 1

Please take a look at the dialogue. When are the underlined phrases used?
下記の対話を見てみましょう。下線部はどのようなときに使われていますか。

Tom: I have been in Japan for about two years.
Yasue: Really? Do you sometimes get homesick?
Tom: Yeah, a little bit.
Yasue: I see. Do you miss your family?
Tom: Yes. I miss my sisters very much. They are like my best friends.
Yasue: Oh, I see.
Tom: Yes. We chat on Zoom every other day.
Yasue: Wow! That's good.

3-2 Communication Tips: Showing Reactions 1

In a conversation, giving a reaction to a speaker helps to show your level of understanding and interest.
会話の中で相槌を打つことは、話し手に自分の理解度や話の内容に対しての興味深さを伝える役割があります。

3-3 Try It Out

Reactions

Yes.	**Really?**	**Wow.**	**That's nice.**	**I see.**	**Great!**	**Uh-huh.**

Practice using the above expressions of "Reactions."
上記の「リアクション」の表現を使う練習をしましょう。

Student A: Read a sentence 1-5 below.
下記の１－５の文を読みます。

Student B: Show a reaction using an expression from above to A. Please use different reactions in this practice.
Ａが一つの文を読んだ後にリアクションをします。なるべく違う種類のリアクションを使いましょう。

Switch the roles of A and B when finished.
その後、ＡとＢの役割を交代しましょう。

Example

Student A: I came to Japan a year ago and I am learning Japanese at school.

Student B: I see.

1. I lived in Singapore for a year when I was an elementary school student.
YOUR REACTION: ______________

2. I have been in Tokyo for a few years. I miss my family very much.
YOUR REACTION: ______________

3. My future goal is to go back and forth between Japan and Australia.
YOUR REACTION: ______________

4. After graduating from university, I would like to go back to my hometown.
YOUR REACTION: ______________

5. I think people in my hometown really care about the community. So, I feel safe living there.
YOUR REACTION: ______________

Part 4 Outcome

Follow the steps below. Then introduce the story of your hometown. Present it with pictures or illustrations.

以下のステップに従ってください。そして、自分の故郷のストーリーを紹介します。写真やイラストを使いながら、以下の手順で紹介してください。

Step 1: **Preparation:** Write down 2 advantages and 2 disadvantages of living in your hometown and explain more with your experiences.

Advantages: ______________________________

____

Your Personal Experience: ______________________________

____

Disadvantages: ______________________________

____

Your Personal Experience: ______________________________

____

Step 2: **Organizing your ideas:** Select the information you would like to talk about from your preparation.

Step 3: **Adding details:** Add more information about your hometown.

Step 4: **Telling your story:** Tell your story to your partner.

Step 5: **Creating visuals:** Introduce your hometown story with pictures and/or illustrations and explain it to your classmates.

Part 5 Reflection

Check your progress. Circle the numbers below.

今回のレッスンを振り返りましょう。下の番号に○を付けましょう。

Now I can ...	☹ ← ---- → ☺
1. talk about the topic of this unit. (my hometown, my friends and family in my hometown)	1---2---3---4---5
2. write about myself using the expressions in Part 2.	1---2---3---4---5
3. use the communication tips in Part 3. (showing reactions)	1---2---3---4---5
4. talk about my personal experience/feelings. (my hometown, my friends and family in my hometown)	1---2---3---4---5

Unit 4 MY FAVORITE FASHION ITEM

Part 1 Exploring the Topic

1-1 First Impression

The Reason to Wear a Black Dress

Profile

Akie has been teaching English to fashion major students in Tokyo. She enjoys teaching English through Coco Chanel's life.

Look at the picture and the title. Write your predictions about the story.
写真とタイトルを見てみましょう。ストーリーについて、あなたの予想を書きましょう。

1-2 Listening

05

Key Words

classy 上品　formal 正式の　plain 装飾のない　reserved 控えめな、遠慮がちな
vivid color 鮮やかな色　mourning 喪中　gaudy 派手な　legendary 伝説的な
essential 必須の　appreciate 感謝する

Listen to the Opening Story and answer the following questions.
オープニングストーリーを聴いて、以下の質問について答えましょう。

1. What item does Akie like and why?
2. Do you like wearing black? Why? Why not?
3. What color clothes do you like to wear? Why?

1-3 Opening Story

Read and check the contents of the Opening Story you heard in the Listening Section.
リスニングで聴いた Opening Story の内容を確認しましょう。

The Reason to Wear a Black Dress

I often wear a black dress. Black makes us look classy and also look stylish. The image of the color black is formal to me. Therefore, I often wear a black dress with a jacket at work. When I wear a plain black dress, I choose a black or white jacket to make myself look reserved. I sometimes choose vivid colors to coordinate with black when I want to look less formal. Also, to look more casual, I wear a bright gaudy scarf.

Black goes well with almost anything. In fact, the black dress has a long history but it became popular as a fashion after American Vogue published a picture of Chanel's Little Black Dress in 1926. Coco Chanel, a legendary international French fashion designer, made the black dress an essential fashion item for women up until the present day. Until that time, black dresses were mainly for people in mourning. Knowing this historical fact makes me appreciate more about wearing a black dress. Fashion evolves just as we do!

*A black dress had originated in the Victorian era as a way to express condolences for the dead, long before the arrival of the Little Black Dress by Chanel.

1-4 Grammar Tips

You can use a basic verb "make" in various situations. Talking about fashion, you can use "make" when you want to express how you look and how you feel because of the clothes you wear.

基本動詞の make を使うと「～を作る」以外に「（ある衣装が）誰かをどう見せる」や「どういう気持ちにさせる」と表現できます。

Example

1. Black **makes** us look classy and also look stylish.
   （黒は私たちを洗練された印象にし、スタイリッシュに見せる）
2. I wear a black or white jacket to **make** myself look reserved.
   （私は控えめな印象を与えるために黒や白のジャケットを着ます）

Part 2 Expressing Yourself

A. Practice writing about yourself in English using some of the expressions below. Use the examples in the parentheses as a reference and change the colored parts into your own words. See Appendix 2 and 3.

下記の表現の型を使って、自分のことを書けるようにしましょう。括弧内の例を参考にして茶色の部分の単語を自分の言葉に置き換えてください。Appendix 2 と 3 を参考にしてください。

お気に入りのファッションアイテム：What's your favorite fashion item and why?

1. I like wearing my **red dress** because it makes me **stand out**.
   (e.g., orange coat, white shirt) (e.g., look outgoing, happy, feel confident)
2. My favorite fashion item is a pair of **gold earrings** as it makes me look **trendy**. (e.g., Nike white sneakers, red glasses) (e.g., pretty, unique, active)

今欲しいファッションアイテム：What fashion item do you want now?

3. I want **an Adidas navy backpack**.
   (e.g., a black tote bag, a big silver ring)
4. I want **a pair of brown loafers**.
   (e.g., a beige jacket, a leather belt)

欲しい理由：Why do you want the item?

5. I want it because **my favorite actor had it**.
(e.g., it looks cool, it goes well with anything)

6. I want them because they will make me **look smarter**.
(e.g., look taller, feel cool)

B. Write about your favorite fashion item and an item you want in English. Use the sentences/phrases/expressions on page 25 and refer to Appendix 3 for fashion items.
上記の文章 / 句 / 表現と Appendix 3 を参考に自分の好きなファッションアイテムについて英語で文章を作りましょう。

Your favorite fashion item: ______________________________

____

A fashion item you want: ______________________________

____

The reason why you want it: ______________________________

____

Part 3 Communication Practice

3-1 Dialogue: Conversation Starters (Giving Compliments)

Please take a look at the dialogue. When are the underlined phrases used?
下記の対話を見てみましょう。下線部はどのようなときに使われていますか。

Ken: I like your outfit today!
Mary: Really? Do you like it?
Ken: Yes, you look good in that yellow dress.
Mary: Thank you, yellow is my favorite color.
Ken: I like it, too. It makes me feel cheerful and energized!
Mary: I like your style, too! You look nice. Your purple shirt suits you.
Ken: Oh, thanks!

3-2 Communication Tips: Conversation Starters (Giving Compliments)

Giving compliments on a person's fashion/items that they are wearing is a great conversation starter.

会話を始める一つの方法として、相手のファッションスタイルや身につけているものについて褒めるとよいでしょう。

3-3 Try It Out

Conversation Starter

Conversation starters	Responses
I like your T-shirt. You look good in yellow. That blouse looks good on you.	Thanks. Thank you! I'm flattered.

Practice using the above expressions of "Conversation Starter."

上記の「カンバセーション・スターター表現」を使う練習をしましょう。

Student A: Compliment your partner's clothing.

相手の着ているものについて褒めてみましょう。

Student B: React to your partner's compliment.

褒められたことに対してリアクションをしましょう。

Switch the roles of A and B when finished.

その後、AとBの役割を交代しましょう。

Example

Student A: Hi, Reiko. I like your T-shirt. It looks good on you.

Student B: Thank you!

Part 4 Outcome

Follow the steps below. Select one fashion item, and introduce the story of the fashion item you want now/your favorite fashion item. Present it with pictures or illustrations.

以下のステップに従ってください。自分の欲しい / お気に入りのファションアイテムを一つ選んで、それについてのストーリーを紹介します。写真やイラストを使いながら、紹介してください。

Step 1: **Brainstorming:** Think about what you want to say about the fashion item you want now/the fashion item you like.

Example: a mind mapping about the fashion item I want now.

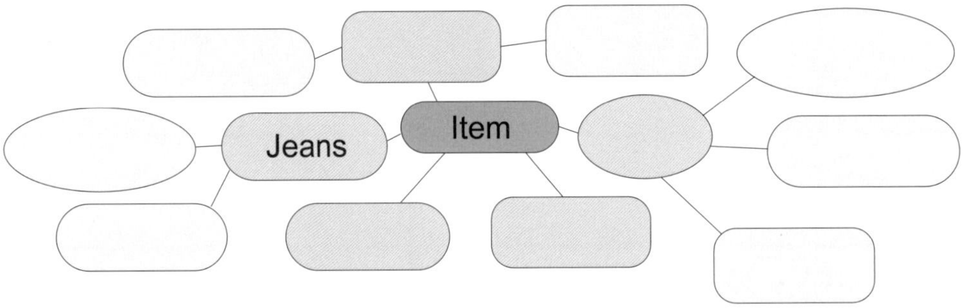

Step 2: **Organizing your ideas:** Decide what item to talk about and come up with the reasons why you like/want it.

Fashion Item	
Reasons	1. 2. 3.

Step 3: **Creating visuals:** Draw or take a picture of the item or bring the item and show it to your classmates when you present.

Step 4: **Talking about your favorite item:** Talk about the fashion item you want now/the fashion item you like and the reasons why you like it. Give at least 2 reasons.

Part 5 Reflection

Check your progress. Circle the numbers below.

今回のレッスンを振り返りましょう。下の番号に○を付けましょう。

Now I can ...	☹ ← ---- → ☺
1. talk about the topic of this unit. (my favorite fashion item)	1---2---3---4---5
2. write about myself using the expressions in Part 2.	1---2---3---4---5
3. use the communication tips in Part 3. (conversation starters: giving compliments)	1---2---3---4---5
4. talk about my personal experience/feelings. (fashion items I want and the reasons)	1---2---3---4---5

Unit 5 DESCRIBING FASHION ITEMS

Part 1 Exploring the Topic

1-1 First Impression

Comfort Is All I Need

Profile

Padi Faraji, who is currently based in Japan, is a visual artist from New Zealand. She lives with her husbamd and her two children. She enjoys Japanese culture and the wabi-sabi mindsent.

Look at the picture and the title. Write your predictions about the story.
写真とタイトルを見てみましょう。ストーリーについて、あなたの予想を書きましょう。

1-2 Listening

06

Key Words

chic 上品な　smart casual 略礼装に近いカジュアルウェア
monochromatic outfits 単色の服装　floral prints 花柄の　a big fan of ~ ～の大ファン
patterned 柄のある　animal prints 動物柄の　fashionista 最新ファッションに敏感な人

Listen to the Opening Story and answer the following questions.
オープニングストーリーを聴いて、以下の質問について答えましょう。

1. What kind of clothes does Padi like to wear?
2. Do you like wearing prints? If so, what kind of prints do you like?
3. What kind of fabrics do you like to wear?

1-3 Opening Story

Read and check the contents of the Opening Story you heard in the Listening Section.
リスニングで聴いた Opening Story の内容を確認しましょう。

Comfort Is All I Need

Hello, my name is Padi. I am a visual artist and I love traveling and learning about other cultures. Even though I like looking neat at all times, I prefer traveling light. I usually carry a small suitcase packed with a few simple items of clothing. While traveling, I like to wear more comfortable clothes made of cotton. I believe with the right choice of comfortable clothes, you can still look chic. In my daily life, I often wear smart casual clothes because it is easier for me to move around and create art. My fashion rules are very simple. Basically, I wear monochromatic outfits and keep to classic styles. I stick to only one piece of jewelry but add special accessories such as a pair of funky sunglasses.

I am not a big fan of prints such as floral prints and animal prints because they are not easy to mix and match with other clothes. I prefer plain outfits. In fact, I'm wearing a white T-shirt and dark navy Chino pants with a bracelet today. My fashionista friend always says, "Learn how to mix patterns properly and you will stand out from the crowd for all the right reasons." Well, I guess I need to learn more about mixing and matching prints.

1-4 Grammar Tips

When you want to describe something that is happening right now, use the present progressive tense with "ing" following a Be verb.

今起こっていることを､「今～している」と表現するときには Be 動詞の次に一般動詞に ing をつけて､現在進行形を使います。

Example

主語 ＋ be 動詞 (am, is, are) ＋ ～ing

1. I **am wearing** a white T-shirt and dark navy Chino pants with a bracelet today.
2. Padi **is painting** at the moment.
3. Yuka **is thinking** about making a skirt.

Part 2 Expressing Yourself

A. Practice writing about yourself in English using some of the expressions below. Use the examples in the parentheses as a reference and change the colored parts into your own words. See Appendix 3 and 5.

下記の表現の型を使って、自分のことを書けるようにしましょう。括弧内の例を参考にして茶色の部分の単語を自分の言葉に置き換えてください。Appendix 3 と 5 を参考にしてください。

あなたが着ている服 : What are you wearing today?

1. I am wearing a **blue polka dot polyester shirt** and a **black plaid skirt** today.
   (color)+(pattern)+(material)+(item) (color)+(pattern)+(item)
2. I am wearing an **orange striped cotton T-shirt** and **black jeans** today.
   (color)+(pattern)+(material)+(item) (color)+(item)

旅行したい場所 : Where are you thinking of going on vacation?

3. I am thinking of going to **Okinawa**.
   (e.g., Hokkaido, Korea, Paris)

そこに持っていくもの : What items are you going to take there?

4. I'm going to take a **brown straw hat** and a **pair of sunglasses** to protect myself from the sun. (e.g., white cotton cap, checked long-sleeved shirt)

5. Also, I am going to take a **pair of purple flip flops** for walking on the beach. (e.g., pair of shorts, floral dress)

Attention! Remember to put a/an before singular nouns. If there is an adjective such as a color or pattern that modifies the noun, put a/an in front of it.
注意！ 単数の名詞の前には a/an を忘れずに入れましょう。名詞を修飾する色や柄などの形容詞がある場合は、その前に a/an を入れます。

B. Write sentences in English about what you are wearing today and about what you are going to take on a trip using the list of expressions above.
上記の文章 / 句 / 表現を参考に自分の着ているもの、旅行で行きたい場所、持ち物について英語で文章を作りましょう。

What are you wearing today? ______________________________

Where are you traveling to? ______________________________

What items are you taking? ______________________________

Part 3 Communication Practice

3-1 Dialogue: Talking about the future

Please take a look at the dialogue. When are the underlined phrases used?
下記の対話を見てみましょう。下線部はどのようなときに使われていますか。

Kai: I'm so excited about our trip to Hawaii. Have you decided what to take?
Janet: Yes! I'm going to take a floral swimsuit and a pair of sunglasses, for sure.
Kai: Nice! What are you going to wear to the concert in the evening?
Janet: Oh. I'm thinking about wearing my black and white cotton mix, polka dot dress.
Kai: Oh, I like that one. How about taking a black cardigan to go with that?
Janet: Right, that's versatile. I will take that one, too! What are you wearing?
Kai: I'm planning to buy a new dress this weekend. Would you like to come with me?
Janet: Sure. I'd love to come with you.

3-2 Communication Tips: Talking about the future

When you express future plans and intentions, you can use “will,” “be going to,” or “be+ing.” Checking the meanings and using them differently will help you convey the situation more accurately.

将来の予定や意思を伝えるときには、will や be going to、be+ -ing を使いますが、どれを使うかで前から決まっていたことなのか、それともその場で決めたことかのニュアンスが変わります。意味を確認して、使い分けるとより正確な状況を伝えることができます。

3-3 Try It Out

Future

Form	Meaning	Example
will	intention 意思、予定	When I get rich, I will visit Paris to buy a Chanel suit.
	just decided その場で決まった予定	You look busy. I will help you.
be going to	already planned すでに決まっている予定	I am going to fly to Honolulu. I’ve booked my flight. I have already made reservations.
be + -ing	already planned (near future) 準備が整った予定	I’m graduating from university this March.

Practice using the above expressions of “Future.”
上記の「未来表現」を使う練習をしましょう。

Student A: Read and then ask the four questions below to your partner.
下記の 4 つの質問を読んでパートナーに質問しましょう。

Student B: Answer the questions using the expressions from above.
質問に答えましょう。必ず未来を表す表現を使って答えましょう。

Switch the roles of A and B when finished.
その後、A と B の役割を交代しましょう。

Example

Student A: What are you going to do this weekend?

Student B: I am going to see the new Spiderman movie with my friend.

Questions

1. What will you do after you graduate from university? (intention)
2. I need your help to finish the assignment. Will you help me? (just decided)
3. Where are you going to work during the summer break? (already planned)
4. What time is your flight leaving for New York? (already planned)

Part 4 Outcome

Follow the steps below to prepare a talk about the fashion items you would like to take on vacation. Talk about the reasons why you will need them there. Present it with pictures or illustrations.

以下のステップに従い、行ってみたい旅行先を決めて、そこに持っていきたいファッションアイテムを紹介しましょう。さらに選んだアイテムがその場所で必要な理由を話しましょう。写真やイラストを使いながら、紹介してください。

Step 1: Brainstorming: Choose a place you would like to visit. Then make a list of fashion items you want to take and decide what to take there. Refer to the table in Appendix 5 and 6.

Preparation: Discuss the questions with your partner.

1. Where would you like to go?

2. What are you going to take there?

3. Give a reason for each item.

Step 2: Creating visuals: Draw a picture of yourself with the outfit and the items, or take a picture of them to show your classmates.

Step 3: Talking about your idea: Talk about the fashion items you want to take to the travel destination and the reasons why you need them.

Part 5 Reflection

Check your progress. Circle the numbers below.

今回のレッスンを振り返りましょう。下の番号に○を付けましょう。

Now I can ...	☹ ← ---- → ☺
1. talk about the topic of this unit. (fashion items: patterns and materials)	1---2---3---4---5
2. write about myself using the expressions in Part 2.	1---2---3---4---5
3. use the communication tips in Part 3. (talking about the future, stating intentions)	1---2---3---4---5
4. talk about my personal experience/feelings. (what I want to take on my trip)	1---2---3---4---5

Unit 6
MY FAVORITE FASHION TRENDS

Part 1 Exploring the Topic

1-1 First Impression

My Favorite
Fashion Trends

Profile

Kim worked as a fashion designer, stylist and illustrator in the UK and Tokyo. She now teaches English and fashion design in arts and fashion universities in Tokyo.

Look at the picture and the title. Write your predictions about the story.
写真とタイトルを見てみましょう。ストーリーについて、あなたの予想を書きましょう。

1-2 Listening

07

Key Words

silhouette シルエット　era 時代　hemlines 裾の線、裾の高さ　reveal 出す、露出する
reflect 反映する　liberate 自由にする、解放する　The Roaring 20s （狂騒の２０年代-アメリカ合衆国でジャズ音楽が台頭して、アールデコが頂点を迎え、生産技術が発達して消費意欲が急激に上昇した戦間期）　alter 仕立て直す　winklepicker １９５０年代に流行った先の長く尖った靴
upcycling アップサイクリング（廃棄物を再利用して新しい製品にアップグレードして変える）

Listen to the Opening Story and answer the following questions.
オープニングストーリーを聴いて、以下の質問について答えましょう。

1. What made Kim become interested in clothes and fashion trends?
2. Have you ever been influenced by your family or relatives close to you?
3. What fashion eras does Kim like? How about you?

1-3 Opening Story

Read and check the contents of the Opening Story you heard in the Listening Section.
リスニングで聴いた Opening Story の内容を確認しましょう。

My Favorite Fashion Trends

My mother was very stylish and fashionable. When my sister and I were very young she often made clothes for us. We loved our home-made dresses. This may be the reason I became interested in clothes and fashion trends. I often watched movies, looked at art, magazines and books to learn more about fashion history and styles. I noticed that the silhouette of women in different eras changed. For example in the 1910s the waistline was small and the shape of the dress was feminine. By the 1920s women's hemlines were shorter and revealed the ankles. The low waistline and the straight silhouette reflected how women had become liberated in society. I think that the "Roaring Twenties" must have been an interesting time to live in.

I also loved the Fifties and Sixties style and I sometimes went through my mother's wardrobe to find fashion items from those eras such as pencil skirts, fitted jackets, and winklepicker shoes. Then I would alter and update the clothes that I found. I frequently went to second-hand clothes shops, flea markets and collected vintage clothes and accessories. Even now I still prefer upcycling rather than buying new clothes and I often wear vintage clothes from the 1950s and 1960s.

1-4 Grammar Tips

When we want to express how often an action is done, we need to use adverbs of frequency.
どのくらいの頻度で物事を行うか詳しく話したい時に、頻度の副詞を使います。

Frequency adverbs 頻度の副詞

100%	always	いつも
	usually	たいてい
	often	よく
	sometimes	時々
	rarely, hardly ever	滅多に〜ない
0%	never	一度もない

主語 (Subject) + 副詞 (Adverb) + 動詞 (Verb)

1. I **usually** wear a T-shirt and jeans when I go to school.

主語 (Subject) + be 動詞 (Be Verb) + 副詞 (Adverb)

2. Sara is **always** cheerful.

Part 2 Expressing Yourself

A. Practice writing about yourself in English using some of the expressions below. Use the examples in the parentheses as a reference and change the colored parts into your own words. See Appendix 7.
下記の表現の型を使って、自分のことを書けるようにしましょう。括弧内の例を参考にして茶色の部分の単語を自分の言葉に置き換えてください。Appendix 7 を参考にしてください。

ファッションの時代のトレンドを説明する：What's your favorite fashion era? Why do you like it?

1. I love the **1910s** fashion era because the shape of the **dress** was **feminine**.
(e.g., 1990s, 2020s) (e.g., skirt, jacket) (e.g., tight and short, big and oversized)

ファッション時代のアイテムの見つけ方：Where do you find the items?

2. I usually buy **vintage Levi's jeans** from **online auction sites**.
(e.g., luxury brand bags, fitted jackets) (e.g., a thrift store, charity shops)

3. I sometimes find **70s chain belts** at **flea markets**.
(e.g., torn jeans, retro beaded cardigans)
(e.g., second hand shops, shops in Kichijoji)

なぜその商品が好きなのですか？：Why do you like the items?

4. I like them because **I saw them in an old movie**.

(e.g., they look expensive, they go with my style)

5. I like them because they will make me **look unique**.

(e.g., more feminine, feel liberated)

B. Write about your favorite fashion era item that you want in English. Where can you find it? Why do you want it? Use the sentences/phrases/expressions above.

上記の文章 / 句 / 表現を参考に自分の好きなファッションアイテムについて英語で文章を作りましょう。

Your favorite fashion era items: ______________________

Where you can find them: ______________________

Why you like them: ______________________

Part 3 Communication Practice

3-1 Dialogue: Checking Understanding

Please take a look at Example 1 and 2. Which conversation is better? Why?

下記の 2 つの対話を見てみましょう。どちらの例が良い対話ですか。なぜでしょうか。

Example 1

Akie: I am interested in the 1920s fashion era because I learned that the liberation of women influenced women's fashion. It's difficult to explain but can you imagine? In just a few years the corset disappeared and hemlines became shorter.

Yohan: ...

Akie: Women achieved freedom in society and the fashion reflected the changes.

Yohan: Umm.

Example 2

Akie: I am interested in the 1920s fashion era because I learned that the liberation of women influenced women's fashion. It's difficult to explain but can you imagine? In just a few years the corset disappeared and hemlines became shorter. Do you follow me?

Yohan: Yes I do. I didn't know that.

Akie: Women achieved freedom in society and the fashion reflected the changes. Do you understand?

Yohan: Yes, I understand. That's interesting.

3-2 Communication Tips: Checking Understanding

By making sure the other person understands what you are saying, you can prevent communication breakdowns.

相手が自分の言ったことを理解したかどうか確かめることでコミュニケーションが途絶えるのを避けることができます。

3-3 Try It Out

Checking Understanding

When you check that you are being understood	When you respond
Do you follow me? Do you understand? Do you know what I mean?	Yes, I do. Sure. Maybe. Can you explain more? Sorry, I don't understand.

Practice using the above expressions of "Checking Understanding." Student A reads the dialogue 1 - 3 below, Student B responds by using the expressions from above.

上記の「相手の理解度を確認する」表現を使う練習をしましょう。Student A が下記の 1 ー 3 の各スクリプトを読んだ後に、上記の表現を使って確認します。Student B は、それに対して返事をします。

Explaining & Checking Understanding	Response
1. **Student A:** I learned in a fashion history class Coco Chanel wore a man's sweater with a belt one day. This started the "flapper look" craze which changed women's fashion forever. **Do you follow me?**	1. **Student B: Sure.**
2. **Student A:** My mother was very stylish and fashionable. When my sister and I were very young she often made clothes for us. We loved our home-made dresses. This may be the reason I became interested in clothes and fashion trends. **Do you understand?**	2. **Student B:**
3. **Student A:** Women's silhouettes in fashion changed with the times. It changed so much from the 20s to the 50s because of many influences such as movies, women's rights and even war. **Do you know what I mean?**	3. **Student B:**

Part 4 Outcome

Follow the steps below. Then introduce the fashion trends of your favorite decade. Present it with pictures or illustrations.

以下のステップに従ってください。そして、自分のお気に入りの年代のファッションついて紹介します。写真やイラストを使いながら紹介してください。

Step 1: Brainstorming: Think of your favorite decade (e.g, 20s,30s etc.) and the fashion styles of that era and create a mind map. Start with the decade as the main topic and then think about any fashion item or trend of that time as subtopics.

Example:

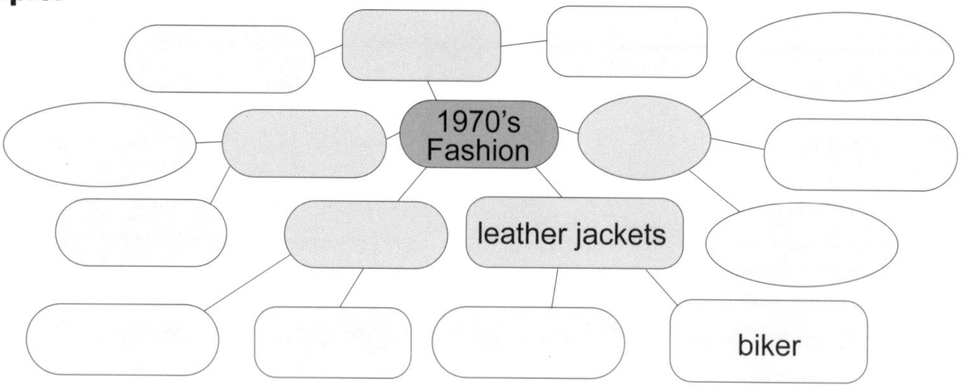

Step 2: Organizing your ideas: Look at your mind map and decide what and how you tell your story about your favorite fashion decade. Select the information you would like to talk about from your mind map.

Step 3: Writing your idea: Write notes about your favorite era and the reasons why you like it. Give examples and describe the trends of that time.

Step 4: Creating visuals: Make a collage or illustration based on your story and explain it to your classmates.

Part 5 Reflection

Check your progress. Circle the numbers below.

今回のレッスンを振り返りましょう。下の番号に○を付けましょう。

Now I can ...	← ---- →
1. talk about the topic of this unit. (favorite trends)	1---2---3---4---5
2. write about myself using the expressions in Part 2.	1---2---3---4---5
3. use the communication tips in Part 3. (checking understanding)	1---2---3---4---5
4. talk about my personal experience/feelings. (my favorite fashion era)	1---2---3---4---5

Unit 7 FASHION AS MY IDENTITY

Part 1 Exploring the Topic

1-1 First Impression

Punk as My Self-Expression

Profile

Kim studied art and fashion design in the UK where Vivienne Westwood taught as a visiting lecturer. As a fashion student, Kim also participated in a weekly music television show in the UK called The Tube that launched many famous artists and had the opportunity to work with Malcolm McLaren.

Look at the picture and the title. Write your predictions about the story.
写真とタイトルを見てみましょう。ストーリーについて、あなたの予想を書きましょう。

1-2 Listening

08

Key Words

mainstream 主流　alternatively 代わりに、代わって　slogans スローガン、標語
social unrest 社会不安　high unemployment 高失業率　inspired 鼓舞された、インスパイヤーされた　provincial 地方の、田舎の　customized 特注の　creative 独創的な

Listen to the Opening Story and answer the following questions.
オープニングストーリーを聴いて、以下の質問について答えましょう。

1. Describe hippy fashion. Do you like hippy fashion?
2. What kind of accessories did punks wear? Why did they wear those accessories?
3. What kind of fashion style expresses your identity? Do you have specific ways to express your identity?

1-3 Opening Story

Read and check the contents of the Opening Story you heard in the Listening Section.
リスニングで聴いた Opening Story の内容を確認しましょう。

Punk as My Self-Expression

The fashion trend that became part of my identity was punk. Punk started in a shop in London, England, in 1976. It was owned and managed by Malcolm McLaren and his girlfriend Vivienne Westwood.

The mainstream fashion in the 1970s was hippy style with flared trousers, long flowing skirts, floral prints, wide-collared shirts, and puffed sleeves. Alternatively, punk fashion included ripped-up T-shirts with shocking slogans, slim drainpipe trousers, torn and covered in safety pins. Hairstyles were Mohican style or spiked up and dyed in bright colors. Punks also wore dog collars, padlocks, chains, studs, and bondage straps as accessories to shock people. Punk was a reaction to the social unrest and high unemployment in the UK at that time. By 1977, punk music and fashion was inspiring young people in provincial towns.

I lived in a provincial town and it was difficult to go to London to buy punk clothes. So I bought second-hand clothes and made clothes from plastic bags, safety pins, ripped-up T-shirts, and customized leather jackets. Punk clothes and music were important ways to express our identity. Finally, punk made us creative and helped us in our future careers. The punk band, The Sex Pistols, cried out "No future" in their song, but punk gave us a future.

*Mohican style (UK) = Mohawk style (US). *Trousers (UK) = pants (US).

1-4 Grammar Tips

When talking about things that happened in the past, the simple past tense is used. Most of the simple past tenses are formed by adding -ed to the end of the verb. Verbs that cannot be made with the -ed suffix are called irregular verbs.

過去に起こった物事について話すときは、単純過去形を使います。単純過去形の多くは動詞の語尾に -ed を付加して作ります。-ed を付加して作れない動詞は不規則動詞と呼ばれます。

Regular Verbs	Add **-ed**	Pronunciation: Final Sound	Irregular Verbs	Different Forms
walk	→ walk**ed**	Voiceless Sound [t]	buy	→ **bought**
watch	→ watch**ed**		eat	→ **ate**
live	→ live**d**	Voiced Sound [d]	see	→ **saw**
sew	→ sew**ed**		wear	→ **wore**
want	→ want**ed**	[t] → [ɪd]	go	→ **went**
need	→ need**ed**	[d] → [ɪd]	teach	→ **taught**

Part 2 Expressing Yourself

A. Practice writing about yourself in English using some of the expressions below. Use the examples in the parentheses as a reference and change the colored parts into your own words. See Appendix 8.

下記の表現の型を使って、自分のことを書けるようにしましょう。括弧内の例を参考にして茶色の部分の単語を自分の言葉に置き換えてください。Appendix 8 を参考にしてください。

好きなファッションスタイルについて：What fashion style do you like to wear?

1. For **streetwear** style, I wear **torn T-shirts and customized leather jackets**.
   (e.g., casual, formal) (e.g., damaged jeans, a black dress)

象徴的なファッションアイテム：What fashion items/accessories do you put on?

2. I put on **safety pins, chains, and studs**.
   (e.g., a pair of big earrings, a choker, a head band)

ファッションアイテムの選択：How do you choose what to wear?

3. I wear **damaged jeans** to/at **a rock concert**, but not to/at **a funeral**.
(e.g., a business suit, a cocktail dress) (e.g., an interview/home) (e.g., a party/a date)

B. Write about your experience with fashion styles using the expressions in Part 2.
上記の文章 / 句 / 表現を参考に自分のファッションスタイルについて英語で文章を作りましょう。

What fashion style do you like? Why?

____

____

Part 3 Communication Practice

3-1 Dialogue: Paraphrasing

Please take a look at the dialogue. When are the underlined phrases used?
下記の対話を見てみましょう。下線部はどのようなときに使われていますか。

Paul: Wow, you look cool in this picture.

Kim: Oh really? We wore clothes that were not mainstream fashion such as ripped-up T-shirts, customized leather jackets, and torn skinny jeans. We called them “drainpipes” back then, For accessories, we would wear safety pins, dog collars, padlocks, chains, studs, and bondage straps so that people would stare at us.

Paul: Do you mean young people started to wear clothes and accessories that shocked?

Kim: Yes. A lot of young people dressed like that to go out to a concert or just to hang out with friends in the UK. It was the perfect style because it shocked older people and it was a reaction to the hard times.

Paul: Are you saying that punk style was a kind of protest against society?

Kim: Yes, that’s right.

3-2 Communication Tips: Paraphrasing

When you want to confirm what a speaker is saying, you can paraphrase. Paraphrasing means to repeat a speaker's idea in clear and simple words and in a different way. You can also paraphrase yourself if others don't understand you.
話し手の言っていることを確認したいときは、言い換えることができます。"Paraphrasing" とは、話し手の考えを簡素化した言葉で、別の表現で繰り返すことです。また、聞き手に理解されない場合は、自分で言い換えることもできます。

3-3 Try It Out

Paraphrasing

Paraphrasing others	Paraphrasing yourself
Do you mean …?	I mean …
So, are you saying that …?	What I am saying is …

Practice using the above expressions of "Paraphrasing."
上記の「パラフレーズ表現」を使う練習をしましょう。

Student A: Read the descriptions below.
下記のの文章を読みます。

Student B: Paraphrase what Student A says.
Student A の言った内容を Student B はパラフレーズします。

Switch the roles of A and B when finished.
その後、A と B の役割を交代しましょう。

Example

Student A: (Read) Christian Dior's "New Look" had a cinched waist and voluminous skirt.

Student B: (Paraphrase) Do you mean Christian Dior designed a completely new silhouette?

Student A: Yes, you are right.

If the paraphrase is not right, you can say …

Student A: (Paraphrase) No, I mean it had a small waist and full skirt.

1. Virgil Abloh combined streetwear and luxury fashion.
2. K-pop fashion style has grown in popularity worldwide.
3. Luxury brand items are extremely costly.

Part 4 Outcome

Follow the steps below. Then share your opinion on what is important when you decide your fashion style. Present it with pictures or illustrations.

以下のステップに従ってください。そして、自分のファッションスタイルを決める上で重要な点について紹介します。写真やイラストを使いながら紹介してください。

Step 1: Brainstorming: Check ✓ the statements below that are true for you and add your own idea about your fashion style.

I like to wear affordable and comfortable clothes.

I like to wear luxury brand clothes.

I want to express my creativity with my style.

It's important to look fashionable.

Your idea: ______________________________

Preparation: What fashion style expresses your character, lifestyle and identity?
Write your ideas about your fashion style and identity by using the expressions below and write the reasons why.

1. I think it is important for me to wear clothes that:
   - **are affordable.**
   - **are comfortable.**
   - **other people think are appropriate.**
   - **make me look fashionable.**
   - **make me stand out.**
   - **are luxury brands.**
   - **express my identity/creativity.**
   - **Your idea:** ______________________________
2. I think/wear ... because ______________________________.
   I don't think/wear ... because ______________________________.

Step 2: Organizing your ideas: Use the sentences from Step 1 and add more about your experience and thoughts on fashion and identity.

Step 3: Telling your story: Tell your ideas/story to your partner.

Step 4: Creating visuals: Make a collage or illustration based on your thoughts/story and explain it to your classmates.

Part 5 Reflection

Check your progress. Circle the numbers below.

今回のレッスンを振り返りましょう。下の番号に○を付けましょう。

Now I can ...	← ---- →
1. talk about the topic of this unit. (fashion styles)	1---2---3---4---5
2. write about myself using the expressions in Part 2.	1---2---3---4---5
3. use the communication tips in Part 3. (paraphrasing)	1---2---3---4---5
4. talk about my personal experience/feelings. (give a talk on my fashion style and identity)	1---2---3---4---5

Unit 8 THE IMPORTANT THINGS

Part 1 Exploring the Topic

1-1 First Impression

Important Things in My Life

Profile

Yumiko Sakamoto taught English at Japanese high schools for 18 years. She currently lives in Austin, Texas with her two teenage daughters and her husband, and teaches English to elementary school students with reading difficulties.

Look at the picture and the title. Write your predictions about the story.
写真とタイトルを見てみましょう。ストーリーについて、あなたの予想を書きましょう。

1-2 Listening

09

Key Words

teaching certificate 教員免許　　end up ~ing （最終的には）～して終わってしまう
depressed 落ち込んでいた、憂鬱になっていた　　tough （仕事などが）とてもつらい、骨の折れる
manage to ~ なんとか～できた　　at this moment 今現在
special education teacher 特別支援教育教員　　passion for ~ ～への情熱

Listen to the Opening Story and answer the following questions.
オープニングストーリーを聴いて、以下の質問について答えましょう。

1. What are the important things in life for Yumiko during her university days and now?
2. What do you expect from your college? Earning a degree and/or making friends?
3. What are the important things in your life now and in the past? Are they the same or different?

1-3 Opening Story

Read and check the contents of the Opening Story you heard in the Listening Section.
リスニングで聴いた Opening Story の内容を確認しましょう。

Important Things in My Life

What are important things for you? Finding an ideal boyfriend or girlfriend? The only important thing during my university days was getting a teaching certificate because I knew I wanted to be an English teacher. However, I ended up skipping many classes because I felt too depressed to do anything at that time. My university days were the toughest times in my life because of many things. However, I managed to graduate and earned a teaching certificate, which allowed me to teach for 18 years in senior high schools in Osaka.

Now, I am a mother of two daughters and I am teaching English as a special education teacher in the U.S. There are two important things in my life right now: the happiness of my daughters and my passion for English education. I want to do my best for my daughters and my work, but it has not been easy keeping a balance between the two.

Now I realize important things in life can change over time and can also stay the same. In my case, “my passion for English education” has remained important throughout my life, but after becoming a parent, it changed. “The happiness of my daughters” became just as important. Have the important things in your life stayed the same or have they changed?

1-4 Grammar Tips

A gerund is a verb that ends in -ing and functions as a noun. For example, “eat (verb)” becomes the gerund in “eating.”

“走ること”や“食べること”のように（〜すること）と言いたいときは、動詞を ~ing 形にすることで名詞化する動名詞を使います。動名詞は名詞なので、文の主語、補語、目的語になります。

Example

eat（食べる）→ eating（食べること）

1. The only important thing during my university days was **getting** a teaching certificate.
（大学時代で唯一重要だったことは教員免許を**得ること**だった）

2. **Becoming** a high school teacher was my dream.
（高校教員に**なること**が私の夢だった）

Part 2 Expressing Yourself

A. Practice writing about yourself in English using some of the expressions below. Use the examples in the parentheses as a reference and change the colored parts into your own words.
下記の表現の型を使って、自分のことを書けるようにしましょう。括弧内の例を参考にして茶色の部分を自分の言葉に置き換えてください。

過去に大切だったこと：What was an important thing for you in the past?

1. The important thing for me when I was **a high school student** (e.g., a 6-year-old girl) was **getting good grades** (e.g., being popular).

今大切なこと：What is the important thing for you now?

2. The important thing for me now is **learning about fashion at my college** (e.g., saving money to study abroad).

過去に大切だったことと今大切なことを比べて：Have the important things in your life changed? Are they the same, different or both the same and different?

3. The important things in my life in the past and right now are **the same**.
(e.g., different, the same, both the same and different)

B. Write about what was important to you in your past and what is important to you now in English using the sentences/phrases/expressions above.
上記の文章 / 句 / 表現を参考に自分の過去に大切だったことについて英語で文章を作りましょう。

The important thing for me in the past: ______________________

____

The important thing/s for me now: ______________________

____

Part 3 Communication Practice

3-1 Dialogue: Agreeing and Disagreeing

Please take a look at Example 1 and 2. Which conversation is better? Why?
下記の 2 つの対話を見てみましょう。どちらの例が良い対話ですか。なぜでしょうか。

Example 1

Chris: Hi, Yumiko. I loved your speech about the important things in life.

Yumiko: Hi, thank you Chris.

Chris: I totally agree with you because important things in life can change over time. Yet some things never change.

Yumiko: Absolutely. The important thing for me was becoming a good teacher and always will be. Now becoming a good parent for my daughters is just as important. I have to find a good balance for both things in my life.

Chris: I see. I hate to disagree with you, but I think family is more important. You want to spend more time with your family.

Yumiko: ..... I'm not sure about that because I want to be a role model for my children. I want to keep working as a teacher and at the same time take care of my children.

Chris: I see that is wonderful.

Example 2

Mike: Hi, Yumiko. I liked your speech about the important things in life.

Yumiko: Hi, thank you Mike.

Mike: I agree that important things in life can change and yet some stay the same. But I don't think that you can keep your work and family life balanced.

Yumiko: Hmm I disagree. It's hard but I do my best because both are just as important to me now.

Mike: Hmm. I see.

3-2 Communication Tips: Agreeing and Disagreeing

As you can see in Example 1, when we have to show disagreement with someone or an idea, it is better to say “I (need to/have to/hate to) disagree with” you so we can soften the comments and avoid conflicts.

Example 1では相手に同意しないときは、はっきりとした断言を避けていることにきがつきましたか？日常会話では圧倒的に“I agree with you”を使いますが､相手に同意しない時には“I (need to/have to/hate to) disagree with you”というように、前に (need to/have to/hate to) などをつけてはっきり断言することを避けることで衝突を避けることができます。

3-3 Try It Out

Agreeing and Disagreeing

Agreeing	Disagreeing
I (totally) agree with you because … That is so true. I also think … That is exactly how I feel because …	I have to disagree with you because … I hate to disagree with you but … I am not sure about that because …

Practice using the above expressions of “Agreeing and Disagreeing.”
上記の「賛成、反対をする」表現を使う練習をしましょう。

Student A: Chooses a topic from the box below and starts the conversation by saying:
“(I think/I believe/In my opinion) the best _______ (topic) is _______ (example) because _______ (reason).”
下記の四角の中からトピックを選んで“(I think/I believe/In my opinion) the best _______ is _______ because _______.” の英文を使って会話を始めます。

Student B: Show agreement or disagreement by using the phrases above with reasons.
賛成か反対かを上記の表の表現を使い、理由を付け加えて言いましょう。

Switch the roles of A and B when finished.
その後、A と B の役割を交代しましょう。

Topics

1. movie **2. anime** **3. comic (manga)** **4. actor**
5. comedian **6. music** **7. drama series** **8. YouTuber**

Part 4 Outcome

Follow the steps below. Then introduce the story of the important things now and in the future. Present it with pictures or illustrations.

以下のステップに従って、自分の 大切なことについて紹介します。写真やイラストを使いながら、以下の手順で紹介してください。

Step 1: **Listing:** Make a list of the things that are important now and things that will be important to you in the future.

Now	**In 10 years**	**In 20 years**

Step 2: **Organizing your ideas:** Decide what and how you tell your story.

Step 3: **Telling your story:** Tell your story to your partner.

Step 4: **Creating visuals:** Make a collage or illustration based on your story and explain it to your classmates.

Part 5 Reflection

Check your progress. Circle the numbers below.

今回のレッスンを振り返りましょう。下の番号に〇を付けましょう。

Now I can ...	☹ ← ---- → ☺
1. talk about the topic of this unit. (important things in my life)	1---2---3---4---5
2. write about myself using the expressions in Part 2.	1---2---3---4---5
3. use the communication tips in Part 3. (agreeing and disagreeing)	1---2---3---4---5
4. talk about my personal experience/feelings. (important things)	1---2---3---4---5

Unit 9 WHAT I LEARNED FROM OTHERS

Part 1 Exploring the Topic

1-1 First Impression

Life-Changing Lessons From My Mentor

Profile

Yumiko Sakamoto graduated from the M.A. TESOL program at San Francisco State University, where she met her life-long mentor. The program is an English teacher program, but the mentor taught her much more than that: life-changing lessons. Throughout the years since then, what she learned from the mentor stays with her and guides her to be a better teacher for her students.

Look at the picture and the title. Write your predictions about the story.
写真とタイトルを見てみましょう。ストーリーについて、あなたの予想を書きましょう。

1-2 Listening

10

Key Words

mentor 師匠、指導者　former professor 大学の恩師　respect 尊敬（する）
admiration 賞賛　mutual 相互の　appreciation 感謝
special needs 特別支援が必要な障がい　ADHD 注意欠陥多動性障がい
learning disability 学習障がい　dyslexia 読字障がい　behavioral issues 問題行動
disrespectful 失礼な

Listen to the Opening Story and answer the following questions.
オープニングストーリーを聴いて、以下の質問について答えましょう。

1. Who is Yumiko's mentor? How did she meet her mentor?
2. Do you have someone who has made a deep impact in your life? If so, who and how did you meet the person?
3. What did you learn from the person?

1-3 Opening Story

Read and check the contents of the Opening Story you heard in the Listening Section.
リスニングで聴いた Opening Story の内容を確認しましょう。

Life-Changing Lessons From My Mentor

I will talk about a mentor who made the biggest impact in my life: Dr. Brown, my former professor at San Francisco State University.

The biggest thing I learned from him is the power of "respect" for his students; he was not just simply nice to his students but showed deep respect and admiration toward them. Through his teaching, I learned that real learning only happens through real relationships and trust between teachers and students; and real relationships can be built only with mutual respect and appreciation. This is very important especially now because I teach many students with special needs such as ADHD, learning disability, and dyslexia. Because of their disabilities, they tend to have a lot of behavior issues, which make their classmates or teachers judge them as "lazy" or "disrespectful" students. It is vital for us not to judge our students by their behaviors, but to understand them by what they really want inside and what is preventing them from trying their best. Our job is to respect and trust them. I learned all of this from Dr. Brown because he trusted us, respected us, and appreciated us, which made all the difference in my life.

1-4 Grammar Tips

When we want to say something more about nouns, we use “who” for a person, “which” for a thing, and “that” for either or both a person and a thing. “Who,” “which,” and “that” are called relative pronouns and they follow right after the nouns that you want to say more about.

人やモノ（名詞）について、さらに詳しく説明したいときに関係代名詞を使います。関係代名詞はその説明したい名詞（先行詞）のすぐ後に置き、その先行詞が人の場合は“who” を使い、先行詞が物の時は“which” を使います。なお関係代名詞“that”は先行詞が人の時も物の時も主格の時も目的格の時も使えます。

Example

1. I will talk about a mentor **who** made the biggest impact in my life.
（私の人生に最も大きな影響を与えた先生について書きます）

2. I have a friend **who** always supports me.
（私にはいつも支えてくれる友がいます）

Part 2 Expressing Yourself

A. Practice writing about yourself in English using some of the expressions below. Use the examples in the parentheses as a reference and change the colored parts into your own words.

下記の表現の型を使って、自分のことを書けるようにしましょう。括弧内の例を参考にして茶色の部分の単語を自分の言葉に置き換えてください。

影響を与えた人の紹介 : The person who made an impact in your life

I will talk about a **teacher** **who** **made the biggest impact in my life:**
(e.g., friend, author) (e.g., changed my life, inspired me)

<**Dr. Brown**>, **my former professor at San Francisco State University**.
<the person's name> (more information about the person)

その人から学んだこと：What did you learn from the person?

The biggest thing I learned from **him** is **the power of "respect" for his students**.
(e.g., her) (e.g., the importance of not giving up)

B. Write about the person in English using the sentences/phrases/expressions above.
上記の文章 / 句 / 表現を参考に自分に影響を与えた人について英語で文章を作りましょう。

The person who made an impact in your life: ______________________________

____

What you learned from the person: ______________________________

____

Part 3 Communication Practice

3-1 Dialogue: Repairing Communication

Please take a look at Example 1 and 2. Which conversation is better? Why?
下記の 2 つの対話を見てみましょう。どちらの例が良い対話ですか。なぜでしょうか。

Example 1

Yumi: Have you heard of a very funny comedian called *Akashiya Sanma*? I believe he is one of the best comedians in Japan.
David: I beg your pardon?
Yumi: *Akashiya Sanma* is the best comedian.
David: *Akashiya Sanma*? I don't know him, but why do you think he is the best?
Yumi: He always makes me laugh. He is not just talented, but he never stops trying something new.
David: I beg your pardon?
Yumi: He makes me laugh and he always tries hard.
David: Pardon?
Yumi: ... Which part didn't you understand?

Example 2

Yumi: Have you heard of a very funny comedian called *Sanma*? I believe he is one of the best comedians in Japan.
David: Could you say that again?
Yumi: *Akashiya Sanma* is the best comedian.
David: *Akashiya Sanma*? I don't know him but why do you think he is the best?
Yumi: He always makes me laugh. He is not just talented, but he never stops trying something new.
David: Can you explain more?
Yumi: Yes, not just funny, he is always trying something new, something that people have never tried before.
David: I see, he never gives up, right?
Yumi: That is right! He is always trying to be better because he loves what he does, making people laugh.

3-2 Communication Tips: Repairing Communication

Using "(I beg your) pardon?" too many times as in Example 1 is not ideal when you do not understand what the other person says to you. To have a natural conversation, you want to use several different phrases to repair communication as shown in the table below.

Example 1のように相手が言ったことが聴き取れなかった場合、"(I beg your) pardon?" ばかりを連呼すると豊かな会話になりません。「もう一度いってくれるかな？」と繰り返しを依頼したり、「それどういう意味？」と説明を依頼したり、「あなたの言ったことはこういうこと？」と相手の言ったことを自分の言葉で言い換えたりするように変化を持たせて聞き返すことで会話が途切れず、しかも相手にとっては自分の話をよく聞いてもらっているという印象も与えます。

3-3 Try It Out

Repairing Communication

Ask for repetition	Ask for explanation
(I beg your) pardon? Could you repeat that, please? What was that again?	What do you mean (by that)? Can you explain more? What does [ ] mean?

Practice using the above expressions of "Repairing Communication."
上記の「会話を修正する」表現を使う練習をしましょう。

Student A: Choose a topic from the box below and talk about the subject that made a great impact on you.
下記の四角の中からトピックを選び、そのトピックで最も影響を与えたものについて英語で伝えましょう。

Student B: (Pretend you did not understand what Student A said) choose a phrase from in the table to repair communication.
Student Aが言ったことが理解できなかった振りをして、上の表にある表現を選んで会話を続けましょう。

Switch the roles of A and B when finished.
その後、AとBの役割を交代しましょう。

Example

Student A: I will talk about a/an comedian who made a great impact on me.
(topic)
That is *Akashiya Sanma*, one of the best comedians in Japan.
(topic)

Student B: Can you explain more?

Topics

1. comedian 2. actor 3. teacher 4. mentor 5. YouTuber
6. athlete 7. artist 8. inventor 9. influencer

Part 4 Outcome

Follow the steps below. Then introduce the story of the person who made a great impact. Present it with pictures or illustrations.

以下のステップに従って、自分に影響を与えた人を紹介します。写真やイラストを使いながら、以下の手順で紹介してください。

Step 1: **Adding more details:** Write a speech script by adding more details to the sentences you wrote in "Expressing Yourself (Part 2, pp. 55-56)."

Step 2: **Telling your story:** Tell your story to your partner.

Step 3: **Revising and creating visuals:** Retell your revised story with more details and visuals, such as pictures of the person, to your class.

Step 4: **Asking questions:** Listen to your classmates' presentation, choose two or three presentations that you would like to ask questions about.

Presenter's Name	Question

Part 5 Reflection

Check your progress. Circle the numbers below.

今回のレッスンを振り返りましょう。下の番号に○を付けましょう。

Now I can ...	☹ ← ---- → ☺
1. talk about the topic of this unit. (what I learned from others)	1---2---3---4---5
2. write about myself using the expressions in Part 2.	1---2---3---4---5
3. use the communication tips in Part 3. (repairing communication)	1---2---3---4---5
4. talk about my personal experience/feelings. (what I learned from others)	1---2---3---4---5

Unit 10 MY FAVORITE PLACE

Part 1 Exploring the Topic

1-1 First Impression

Profile

Roozbeh Zaroodi was born and raised in Tehran, Iran. He worked as a construction engineer for four years after college in Iran. Currently, he is studying English at California State University.

Look at the picture and the title. Write your predictions about the story.
写真とタイトルを見てみましょう。ストーリーについて、あなたの予想を書きましょう。

1-2 Listening

11

Key Words

construction management コンストラクション・マネジメント、施工管理
be obsessed with ~ ～に夢中になる　improve 改善する　route 道、ルート
magnificent 素晴らしい、壮大な　breathtaking 息をのむほど美しい
encouragement 激励、励まし　relieve 和らげる、軽減する
remind 人 of ~ 人に～を思い出させる　feel grateful 感謝する、ありがたく思う

Listen to the Opening Story and answer the following questions.
オープニングストーリーを聴いて、以下の質問について答えましょう。

1. What is the place where Roozbeh keeps going back?
2. Do you have such a place? If so, what is that place and why do you go back there?

1-3 Opening Story

Read and check the contents of the Opening Story you heard in the Listening Section.
リスニングで聴いた Opening Story の内容を確認しましょう。

My Favorite Place

Do you have any favorite places where you keep going back?

I am Roozbeh, and I am an international student in California. I recently moved from Iran to study construction management. Nowadays, I am obsessed with studying English and preparing myself to take the TOEFL exam. I am trying to improve my English as quickly as possible. When I feel stressed about the exam, I feel the need to take care of myself.

To take care of my soul, body, and mind, I often go to a beautiful hill near the university campus. There is a route where I usually walk and see this magnificent view. From there, you can see a wide view of San Francisco Bay. It is breathtaking. Whenever I go there, it improves my mood, and I feel relaxed. There, I usually call my family because I miss them, and I want to share this beautiful view with them. During the phone call, they motivate me by giving me advice and encouragement. They inspire me to keep going.

This is a place where I relieve my stress and feel connected to my family and nature. I believe that the scenery will forever remind me of the hard work and difficulties I had. I am always grateful for everything that I have in my life, and right now I feel especially grateful that I am starting my new life at such a lovely place.

1-4 Grammar Tips

"Where" can be used to describe a place. For example, if you want to say "a place where you keep going back," you say "a place" first and then add the explanation later. The explanation pattern is: where + subject + verb. In this case, "you keep going back" is added at the end. Here, "where" acts as a glue word to connect the place and its description. This "where" is called a relative adverb.

Where を使うと場所の説明ができます。例えば、「あなたがくり返し行く場所」と言いたい時は、まず a place と先に言って、説明を後につけ加えます。説明の順番は、where + 主語＋動詞で、ここでは「あなたがくり返し行く」＝ you keep going back を最後に付け足します。ここでの where は、場所とその説明をつなぐ接着剤のような役割をしていて、「どこ？」という意味はありません。このような where を関係副詞といいます。

Do you have a place (**where** you keep going back)?
（あなたがくり返し行く場所）

(place) (subject) (verb)
Example: 場所 + (**where** + 主語 + 動詞)

1. There is a route (**where** I usually walk and see this magnificent view).
（私がいつも歩いてこの素晴らしい景色を見る道）
2. This is a city (**where** I grew up). （私が育った市）
3. I like to eat at a restaurant (**where** chefs cook in front of me).
（シェフが目の前で料理してくれるレストラン）

Part 2 Expressing Yourself

A. Practice writing about yourself in English using some of the expressions below. Use the examples in the parentheses as a reference and change the colored parts into your own words.
下記の表現の型を使って、自分のことを書けるようにしましょう。括弧内の例を参考にして茶色の部分の単語を自分の言葉に置き換えてください。

あなたの好きな場所：What is your favorite place?

1. My favorite place is **a beautiful hill** near **my university**.
(e.g., a restaurant, a park, Tokyo Midtown) (e.g., my house, <Fukuoka> Station)

そこで何をする？：What do you do there?

2. It is a **place** where **I often call my family**.
   (e.g., coffee shop, museum) (e.g., I enjoy chatting with my friends, I met my boyfriend)

好きな理由：Why do you like that place?

3. I like the **hill** because **I feel connected to my family and nature**.
   (e.g., lake, shrine) (e.g., I have a great memory with my grandparents, I used to visit there when I was a child)

B. Write about your favorite place in English using the sentences/phrases/expressions above.
上記の文章 / 句 / 表現を参考に自分の好きな場所について英語で文章を作りましょう。

Your favorite place: ______________________________

What do you do there? It is a place where ______________________________

____

Why do you like that place? ______________________________

Part 3 Communication Practice

3-1 Dialogue: Showing Reactions 2

Please take a look at the dialogue. When are the underlined phrases used?
下記の対話を見てみましょう。下線部はどのようなときに使われていますか。

[Sophia is showing photos on her cellphone to Hajime.]

Hajime: Wow, look at you! You look amazing! Are you dancing?

Sophia: Yeah, this is my favorite dance studio. It's a place where my friends and I practice dancing every week.

Hajime: Oh, are you on a dance team?

Sophia: Hmm, not really. We just like to get together. This is a place where anyone can come and have fun. I like this studio because I can meet new people there.

3-2 Communication Tips: Showing Reactions 2

Reaction words such as Wow, Yeah, Oh, Hmm are quite useful in English conversation. By using these short words, not only can you express your emotion instantly, but also the reaction words can buy you time to think about what you are going to say next.

Wow, Yeah, Oh, Hmmm など Reaction Words（= あいづち）は英会話の時にとても便利！ この短い言葉を入れるだけで、あなたの感情を簡単に表現できるだけではなく、それを言っている間に次に話す言葉を考える時間も稼げるので、とても便利です。

3-3 Try It Out

Showing Reactions 2

Wow, Oh = 驚き、感嘆を表現	**Hmm** = 考え中、何かを言いにくい時
Yeah = Yes のカジュアルな表現	**Oops** = 失敗した時
Well =「ええと」	**Ouch** = 痛い時、痛そうな時
I see =「なるほど」	**Eww** = 気持ち悪いものを見た時
Aww = 可愛い人や物を見た時	**Yay** = お祝いしたい時

Practice using the above expressions of "Showing Reactions 2."
上記の「リアクション 2」の表現を使う練習をしましょう。

Both Student A and B need to fill in the blanks and complete the conversation. Please use different reactions in this practice.
A も B も空欄を埋めて会話を完成させましょう。なるべく違う種類のリアクションを使いましょう。

Switch the roles of A and B when finished.
その後、A と B の役割を交代しましょう。

Example

Student A: I'm getting married this spring!

Student B: Wow / Oh / Yay! I'm happy for you!

1. **Student A:** _________! You are stepping on my foot!
   Student B: _________. Sorry.
2. **Student A:** Look at this cute little puppy! **Student B:** _________ …
3. **Student A:** Are you available tomorrow?
   Student B: _________, let me check my schedule.
4. **Student A:** I just passed the English exam.
   Student B: _________! Congratulations!
5. **Student A:** _____! That guy is throwing up on the street. **Student B:** _________.

Part 4 Outcome

Follow the steps below. Then introduce the story of your favorite place from your hometown. Present it with pictures or illustrations.

以下のステップに従ってください。そして、自分の好きな場所のストーリーを紹介します。写真やイラストを使いながら、以下の手順で紹介してください。

Step 1: **Brainstorming:** Think of all the places you enjoy visiting. After brainstorming, pick one place for your story telling.

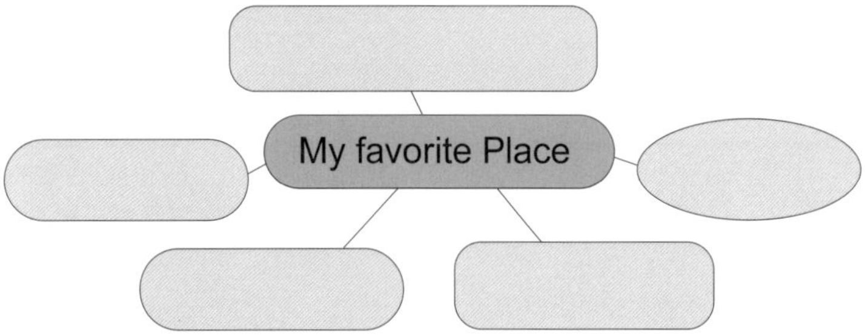

Step 2: **Organizing your ideas:** Write about the place answering the questions below.

1. What is your favorite place? ____________________
   What is the name of the place? ____________________
   Where is it? ____________________
2. What do you do there? ____________________
   When do you go? ____________________
   Who goes there with you? ____________________
   Describe a special memory you had at that place.
   ____
3. Why do you like the place? Why is it special or important for you?
   ____

Step 3: **Creating visuals:** Find a photo of your favorite place or draw it.

Step 4: **Talking about your favorite place:** Share the photo of your favorite place on a projector or online, and describe it in pairs/groups or to class.

Part 5 Reflection

Check your progress. Circle the numbers below.

今回のレッスンを振り返りましょう。下の番号に○を付けましょう。

Now I can ...	← ---- →
1. talk about the topic of this unit. (my favorite place)	1---2---3---4---5
2. write about myself using the expressions in Part 2.	1---2---3---4---5
3. use the communication tips in Part 3. (showing reactions)	1---2---3---4---5
4. talk about my personal experience/feelings. (my favorite place)	1---2---3---4---5

Unit 11 TRANSPORTATION

Part 1 Exploring the Topic

1-1 First Impression

Commuting Time

Profile

Narumi Ujita graduated from the M.A. TESOL program at San Francisco State University in 2004. After working for a company for many years, she decided to dedicate her life to language education. Currently, she enjoys teaching both English and Japanese. She is also a mother of two sons.

Look at the picture and the title. Write your predictions about the story.
写真とタイトルを見てみましょう。ストーリーについて、あなたの予想を書きましょう。

1-2 Listening

12

Key Words

pregnant 妊娠した　pregnancy 妊娠期間　commute 通勤（通学）する
transport hub 交通の中心　transfer 乗り換える　belly お腹
maternity tag 妊娠ストラップ　cellphone (smart phone) 携帯電話

Listen to the Opening Story and answer the following questions.
オープニングストーリーを聴いて、以下の質問について答えましょう。

1. How did Narumi feel when some kind people gave up their seats for her?
2. Do you think you should give up your seat on the train for others?
3. If so, who do you give up your seat for? If not, why not?

1-3 Opening Story

Read and check the contents of the Opening Story you heard in the Listening Section.
リスニングで聴いたOpening Storyの内容を確認しましょう。

Commuting Time

Today, I saw a pregnant woman sitting in the bus, and that reminded me of the kindness which I had received during my pregnancy. When I was pregnant with my first child, I used to commute for eighty minutes to work one way. First, I walked to the nearest bus stop, and took a bus to the subway station. Next, I took the subway to Umeda Station, the largest transport hub in Osaka. Then, I transferred and took a train to the station where I worked. It was truly a long way. Even though I was a healthy pregnant lady, I felt tired standing all the way. Therefore, I tried to get on the train from the doors near the priority seats. On such days, some kind people gave up their seats for me, when they saw my belly and the maternity tag hanging from my bag. I felt grateful when people gave up their seats for me.

People who commute are very tired, especially on the way home, after school or work. Some people are sleeping in the train and others are checking their mobile phones. Some may want to give up their seats to the people in need. Others may not want to give up their seats to anyone. I just wish that more people would care about the people nearby.

1-4 Grammar Tips

By using the term "when", we can set the scene and tell what happened at that time. 'When' is used as a conjunction here.

when を使って、「〜とき」と場面設定をして、そのときに何が起こったかを伝えることができます。ここでの when は接続詞です。

Example

When I was pregnant with my first child, I used to commute for eighty minutes to work one way.

Notice that a comma is used to separate two clauses when the adverb clause comes first. The meaning is exactly the same in both sentences below.

接続詞で文を始める場合は、コンマ（,）で区切ります。接続詞の節が文の途中に入る場合は、コンマは不要です。どちらも意味は同じです。

When the phone rang, the baby woke up.（電話が鳴った時、赤ちゃんが起きた）
The baby woke up **when** the phone rang.（電話が鳴った時、赤ちゃんが起きた）

Part 2 Expressing Yourself

A. Practice writing about yourself in English using some of the expressions below. Use the examples in the parentheses as a reference and change the colored parts into your own words.

下記の表現の型を使って、自分のことを書けるようにしましょう。括弧内の例を参考にして茶色の部分の単語を自分の言葉に置き換えてください。

移動手段ついて話す表現：How do you go to school?

1. I go to school by **train**. (e.g., bus, subway)
2. I **walk** to school. (e.g., bike, drive)
3. I take the **train** to school. (e.g., bus, subway, JR Line)

乗り換えに関する表現：Do you need to change the lines?

4. Yes, I **change lines** at <**Shinagawa**> Station.
(e.g., transfer)
No, it's only one train ride from <**Yokohama**> Station to <**Meguro**> Station.

移動中にすること : What do you do on the train/bus/subway?

5. I usually **check my emails** on the train.
   (e.g., text message to my friends, read a book, check the news online, sleep)

通勤・通学中の経験 : Can you tell a story of your commuting time?

6. Passengers **talk in a low voice**. (e.g., are quiet and close their eyes)
7. I hesitated to **give up my seat** because I **don't like to talk to strangers**.
   (e.g., chat with my friends, answer the phone) (e.g., consider it as bad manners)
8. **A foreign traveler** asked me the directions **in English**.
   (e.g., A man, A lost child) (e.g., to the post office, to the information desk)
9. **The train was delayed** due to **an accident**.
   (e.g., I was stuck in a train, I was late) (e.g., heavy snow, an electrical system trouble)

B. Write the directions from your home to school/work, the way you spend the time, and your experience during commuting time using the sentences/phrases/expressions above.
上記の文章/句/表現を参考に自宅から学校や職場までの行き方、通学・通勤中の過ごし方や経験したことを英語で書きましょう。

How do you go to school/work? ______________________________

What do you do during the commuting time? ______________________________

The experience or event during the commuting time: ______________________________

____

Part 3 Communication Practice

3-1 Dialogue: Small Talk

Please take a look at the dialogue below. When are the underlined phrases used?
下記の対話を見てみましょう。下線部はどのようなときに使われていますか。

Example 1

Narumi: Hey, have you finished the assignment from last week?

Ken: Actually I haven't. How about you?

Narumi: No, I spent three hours last night but I couldn't finish it.

Ken: Yeah, same here. It was too difficult for me.

Example 2

Jack: It's hot and humid today. I hate summer!

Yasue: Yeah, you don't want to go outside.

Jack: I will stay in the classroom all day!

3-2 Communication Tips: Small Talk

Small talk is a type of conversation that is less serious and you can use to break the ice with strangers. It helps to relieve tension, get closer to the other person, and find common ground to build relationships. It can be used with classmates who sit nearby in the classroom, with people nearby while waiting for the bus, or with people who are at the same table in a business meeting.

スモールトークは「雑談」や「世間話」と訳されることがあります。深刻ではないトピックを選んで、あまり知らない者同士が会話を通して心地よい時間を過ごします。これは緊張を和らげたり、相手との距離を縮めたり、共通点を見出したりして人間関係を築くのに役立ちます。教室で近くに座ったクラスメイトや、バスの待ち時間に居合わせた人や、もしくはビジネスで同席した人との間で活用できます。

3-3 Try It Out

Small Talk: possible topics to start a small talk

Topics	Possible Questions	Possible Responses
Transportation	How do you come to school?	I walk to school. My house is really close.
Time	Why are you so early today?	I wanted to ask some questions about homework to our teacher.
School/Class	Did you finish your homework?	Yes, I did. How about you?
Weather	It's a nice day today.	Yeah, I should go somewhere after school.

Practice using the above expressions of "Small Talk." Student A chooses a topic from the box below and says to Student B, "Let me choose (Topic)." Student A starts a small talk with the topic and Student B continues the talk.

上記の「スモールトークを始める」表現を使う練習をしましょう。Student A が下記の四角の中からトピックを選び、Student B に対してそのトピックに関するスモールトークを始めてください。Student B も話を続けてください。

Example

Student A: Let me choose "transportation." How did you come to school?

Student B: I took three trains, the Odakyu Line, the Yamamote Line and the Nanboku Line.

Student A: That's a lot. It must take a long time to get here.

Topics

1. transportation **2. weather** **3. assignments** **4. food** **5. your idea**

Part 4 Outcome

Follow the steps below. Then tell how you came to school today, and how you went to your favorite place last time. Present it with pictures or illustrations.

以下のステップに従ってください。そして、自分の家から学校までの道のりと、学校からお気に入りの場所への道のりを英語で説明しましょう。写真やイラストを使いながら以下の手順で話してください。

Step 1: **Preparation:** Discuss the questions with your partner.

1. How do you go to school?

   ____

2. Do you need to change trains?

   ____

Step 2: **Organizing your ideas:** Write down your experience during commuting time.
1) what you saw on the way 2) what you did/felt.

What you saw on the way: ______________________________

____

What you did/felt: ______________________________

____

Step 3: **Telling your story:** Tell your story to your partner.

Part 5 Reflection

Check your progress. Circle the numbers below.

今回のレッスンを振り返りましょう。下の番号に○を付けましょう。

Now I can ...	☹ ← ---- → ☺
1. talk about the topic of this unit. (commuting time)	1---2---3---4---5
2. write about myself using the expressions in Part 2.	1---2---3---4---5
3. use the communication tips in Part 3. (small talk)	1---2---3---4---5
4. talk about my personal experience/feelings. (commuting time)	1---2---3---4---5

Unit 12 MY PASSION

Part 1 Exploring the Topic

1-1 First Impression

© Dai Sugano

Profile

Makiko Muto taught English at a high school in Nagoya for six years. After completing the M.A. TESOL program at San Francisco State University, she has been teaching English to international students at California State University.

Look at the picture and the title. Write your predictions about the story.
写真とタイトルを見てみましょう。ストーリーについて、あなたの予想を書きましょう。

1-2 Listening

13

Key Words

stick with ~　〜にくっつく → (人) をとりこにする　　senior coworker　職場の先輩
feel passionate about ~　〜に夢中・熱心である　　turn + (数字)　(数字) 歳になる
even though 主語＋動詞　〜だけれども　　last (v)　続く
too old to ~　〜するのに年を取り過ぎている　　give up ~ing　〜するのをあきらめる

Listen to the Opening Story and answer the following questions.
オープニングストーリーを聴いて、以下の質問について答えましょう。

1. How did Makiko find her passion?
2. Do you have a passion for something? If so, what is it? If not, do you think you will find one someday?

1-3 Opening Story

Read and check the contents of the Opening Story you heard in the Listening Section.
リスニングで聴いた Opening Story の内容を確認しましょう。

Finding a Passion

Do you have a passion for something? If not, do you know how to find your passion?

As a child, I tried several sports and hobbies, but nothing really stuck with me. When I first started working, my senior coworker asked me, "Do you have anything you feel passionate about?" I said, "Not really.", and his reply surprised me: "You will probably find one by the time you turn forty."

I did not believe him at all because I thought I was the kind of person who could not get passionate about anything. I also thought finding a passion is only for young people. After becoming an adult, all you do is to work and maybe take care of your family. That was what I believed at that time.

Even though I did not believe him, I kept on trying new things, such as traveling and volunteering. Everything was fun, but nothing lasted until one day I found a sign at a shopping mall which said "free tango lessons on Sundays." I followed the sign and it led me to a big outdoor space. It was on the first floor and right next to a big water fountain.

On the next Sunday, I went back to the same place to take my first tango lesson. Ever since then, tango has become my passion. Now I strongly believe that you can never be too old to find your passion. If you do not know what to do in your life, try something new and never give up searching for your passion.

1-4 Grammar Tips

You can create a noun phrase by combining a question word (QW), a subject (S), and a verb (V). Once you get used to this word order, you can ask many different kinds of questions.

「あなたは何がしたいのか」「あなたの好きなミュージシャンは誰なのか」「図書館はどこか」などの意味の塊は、疑問詞、主語、動詞をつなげるだけで作ることができます（＝名詞句）。それによりあなたの質問の幅が広がります。

Example

(QW) (S) (V)

疑問詞 ＋ 主語 ＋ 動詞

1. Do you know **what** you want to do?（あなたは何がしたいのか）
2. Can you tell me **who** your favorite musician is?（あなたの好きなミュージシャンは誰なのか）
3. Could you tell me **where** the library is?（図書館はどこか）

Part 2 Expressing Yourself

A. Practice writing about yourself in English using some of the expressions below. Use the examples in the parentheses as a reference and change the colored parts into your own words.

下記の表現の型を使って、自分のことを書けるようにしましょう。括弧内の例を参考にして茶色の部分の単語を自分の言葉に置き換えてください。

自分が情熱を注いできた / これから注ぎたい事柄 : What are you passionate about?

1. I'm **passionate about dancing tango**.
   (e.g., crazy about, into) (e.g., making bags, K-pop, American dramas, playing soccer)
2. I'd like to start learning **Spanish**.
   (e.g., knitting techniques, how to create a good YouTube channel)

それを知ったきっかけ : How did you get to know about it?

3. **One of my friends** taught me.
   (e.g., my brother, my mother, my high school teacher)
4. I happened to see **a documentary movie** about **hip-hop dance**.
   (e.g., an online video clip, an advertisement on the train) (e.g., swimming, kimono)

その活動をする場所 : Where do you go to do that?

5. I usually go to **a studio** in <**downtown San Francisco**>.
   (e.g., my friend's house, a stadium, a gym)

B. Write about yourself in English using the sentences/phrases/expressions above.
上記の文章 / 句 / 表現を参考に自分について英語で文章を作りましょう。

What are you passionate about? ______________________________

How did you get to know about it? ______________________________

Where do you go to do that? ______________________________

Part 3 Communication Practice

3-1 Dialogue: Describing Locations

Please take a look at the dialogue below. When are the underlined phrases used?
下記の対話を見てみましょう。下線部はどのようなときに使われていますか。

Amy: Hello ... do you have a moment? Do you know where Kitty Cat Cafe is?

Akira: Sure. Do you see the convenience store across the street? The Cat Cafe is on the second floor.

Amy: Thanks!

[Inside the cafe]

Amy: Excuse me, can you tell me where I can pay the admission fee?

Kota: Do you see the vending machine? It's behind the glass door. You can buy the admission ticket from that machine.

Amy: Do you know where I should leave my jacket and bag?

Kota: There is a locker. It's next to the restroom.

Amy: Well ... then could you tell me where the restroom is?

Kota: It's at the end of this hallway. You will see it on your left.

Amy: Thanks! Oh, I can't wait to play with the cute cats!

3-2 Communication Tips: Describing locations

These days we can search directions on our smartphone easily, however, in reality sometimes you get lost even if you are near the destination. In that case, you may want to use the following expressions shown in 3-3 Try It Out to describe the exact location effectively.

最近は、どこに行くときもスマートフォンですぐに行き方を調べることができます。しかし、実際は、目的地周辺に着いてからも迷うことがあります。その時は 3-3 Try It Out のような表現を使って位置関係を伝えるとわかりやすくなります。

3-3 Try It Out

Prepositions of Locations

It is on the first/second/third floor.	1，2，3 階にある
It is in front of A.	A の前にある
It is next to A.	A の隣にある
It is behind A.	A の後ろにある
It is close to A.	A の近くにある
It is across from A.	A の向かいにある
It is on the left/right.	左 / 右側にある

Practice using the above expressions of "Prepositions of Locations." You can use the map in Appendix 9 or your own school site.

上記の「位置関係を示す前置詞」の表現を使う練習をしましょう。Appendix 9 の地図、または自分の学校について説明しましょう。

Example

Student A: (Do you know/Can you tell me/Could you tell me) where the gym is?

Student B: Yes, it's over there **next to** Parking A.

Places

1. gym　2. library　3. cafeteria　4. admission office　5. your idea

Part 4 Outcome

Follow the steps below. Then introduce the story of your passion. Present it with pictures or illustrations.

以下のステップに従ってください。そして、あなたが情熱を注いでいること、またはこれから情熱を注いでみたいことについてのストーリーを紹介します。写真やイラストを使いながら、以下の手順で紹介してください。

Step 1: **Brainstorming:** Write your ideas about things you are passionate about or things you want to try. You can use a "listing" technique for brainstorming.

Example:

Things that I am passionate about/ I want to try

✓ ______

✓ ______

✓ ______

Choose one or two ideas that you want to tell more about from your list.

Preparation: Discuss the questions with your partner.

1. What are you passionate about or is there anything you want to try?
2. How did you find out about it?
3. Why do you love it or why do you want to try it?
4. Where do you do the activity and how do you get there?

Step 2: **Organizing your ideas:** Organize what and how you tell the story of your passion. Write them down if necessary.

Step 3: **Finding an image:** Find a photo or illustration of the activity you want to describe.

Step 4: **Telling your story:** Tell the story about how you found your passion with the image in pairs/groups or to class.

Part 5 Reflection

Check your progress. Circle the numbers below.

今回のレッスンを振り返りましょう。下の番号に○を付けましょう。

Now I can ...	☹ ← ---- → ☺
1. talk about the topic of this unit. (my passion)	1---2---3---4---5
2. write about myself using the expressions in Part 2.	1---2---3---4---5
3. use the communication tips in Part 3. (prepositions of locations)	1---2---3---4---5
4. talk about my personal experience/feelings. (my passion)	1---2---3---4---5

Unit 13 FINDING MY INNER PEACE

Part 1 Exploring the Topic

1-1 First Impression

Zen as a Path for Healing

Profile

Tracy Cramer graduated from the San Francisco State University MA TESOL program in 2001. He lived in Japan and taught English at a university in Osaka for 11 years. He has practiced Zen Buddhism for 27 years. He currently lives in Austin, the capital city of Texas, USA.

Look at the picture and the title. Write your predictions about the story.
写真とタイトルを見てみましょう。ストーリーについて、あなたの予想を書きましょう。

1-2 Listening

14

Key Words

meditation 瞑想　COVID-19 コロナ　Buddhism 仏教　anxiety 心配・不安
depression 憂うつ　monk 僧侶　monastery 僧院ー仏道修行する場所
vow to 動詞の原形 ～する誓いを立てる　I am grateful that ~ ～に感謝している
paths 道、方法

Listen to the Opening Story and answer the following questions.
オープニングストーリーを聴いて、以下の質問について答えましょう。

1. Have you ever tried meditation before? If so, did it help you calm down, or how did it help you? If not, do you want to try it?
2. What do you do to relieve stress or anxiety?

1-3 Opening Story

Read and check the contents of the Opening Story you heard in the Listening Section.
リスニングで聴いた Opening Story の内容を確認しましょう。

Zen as a Path for Healing

Facing a wall and sitting on a zafu（座布）, a special cushion for zazen（座禅）, I sit in meditation for 40 minutes every morning. Since COVID-19 hit, I have been sitting with people from many parts of the United States as well as other countries such as Australia on Zoom.

It has been 27 years since I started practicing Zen Buddhism. When I encountered Zen, I did not know it was a kind of Buddhism, but I knew meditation was one of the best ways to slow down the mind in order to understand myself better and to feel less anxiety or depression. It worked for me and helped me survive the difficulties I had at that time. It was difficult to do at first because the teachers always told us we must not move and that we have to let go of thoughts. However, little by little, I could do these things. Then, over time, I became better friends with my thoughts and feelings. That gave me more inner peace. It was so helpful that I decided to deepen my practice by becoming a Zen monk at a monastery in

California. After several years of training, I received my monk name, which means “I vow to follow Buddha’s Way of living in harmony with others and the world.”

I am grateful that I found Zen and grateful that there are many paths of healing in this world.

1-4 Grammar Tips

We use present perfect (have + past participle of a verb) to express an event that happened in the past and has present consequences. While past tense indicates a point in the past, present perfect indicates a link between a point in the past and now; therefore, present perfect cannot be used with words or phrases which indicate a point in the past such as “yesterday” or “2 years ago.”

過去から始まった動作や状態が今も続いていること（例：東京に 5 年間住んでいます）や、これまでに経験したこと（例：沖縄に行ったことがあります）などを表すときに、have/has + 動詞の過去分詞形を使い、これを現在完了形といいます。過去のある一時点のみを表す過去時制とは異なり、過去と現在をつなげた幅のある表現なので、過去のある一時点を表す語句 (例：yesterday, 2 years ago, when I was young) とは共に使えないことに注意しましょう。

Example

1. I **have** **been** sitting and meditating with people from many parts of
   have 過去分詞形
   the United States.

2. It **has** **been** 27 years since I started practicing Zen Buddhism.
   have 過去分詞形　　since の後ろは過去形

Part 2 Expressing Yourself

A. Practice writing about yourself in English using some of the expressions below. Use the examples in the parentheses as a reference and change the colored parts into your own words.
下記の表現の型を使って、自分のことを書けるようにしましょう。括弧内の例を参考にして茶色の部分の単語を自分の言葉に置き換えてください。

不安になる / 緊張する状況：When do you have anxiety?

1. I become **anxious** when I am not ready for a **test**.
   (e.g., worried, nervous)　(e.g., presentation, date)

2. I have difficulty **breathing** when I’**m in a crowded train**.
   (e.g., speaking, concentrating)　(e.g., talk in public, am in a busy cafe)

不安や緊張を取り除く方法：How do you destress?

3. "Listening to music" has been my way of relieving stress since I was a child.
(e.g., reading comics, watching movies)　(e.g., 2015, I broke up with my ex-boyfriend)

不安や緊張した時に使うもの・やること：What do you do to relax?

4. I listen to my favorite artist's songs such as <Yonezu Kenshi and Maroon 5>.
(e.g., read, watch)　(e.g., author's books, director's movie)

B. Write about what you do when you are anxious or worried using the sentences/phrases/expressions above.

上記の文章 / 句 / 表現を参考にあなたが不安だったり緊張した時にすることについて英語で文章を作りましょう。

When do you have anxiety or feel worried? ______________________________

What do you do to get rid of anxiety and worries? ______________________________

____

Do you have a special hobby or place to relax/destress? ______________________

____

Part 3 Communication Practice

3-1 Dialogue: Giving Instructions

Please take a look at Example 1 and 2. Which conversation is better? Why?

下記の 2 つの対話を見てみましょう。どちらの例が良い対話ですか。なぜでしょうか。

Example 1

Tracy: I would like to share my way of relieving stress.

Yumi: Sure, let's hear it.

Tracy: First, sit down in a comfortable position with your back straight. And then notice your breathing: in and out, in and out. Keep breathing. Focus on your breathing, nothing else. Do you feel that you are calming down? If so, you are meditating.

Yumi: …?

Example 2

Tracy: I would like to share my way of relieving stress.

Yumi: Sure, let's hear it.

Tracy: First, please sit down in a comfortable position with your back straight.

Yumi: Yes.

Tracy: And then, try to notice your breathing: in and out, in and out. Got it?

Yumi: I am doing it.

Tracy: Good. Please keep breathing. Focus on your breathing, nothing else.

3-2 Communication Tips: Giving Instructions

Which dialogue is better? In Example 2, Tracy pauses after each instruction to make sure Yumi understands.
会話例 2 では Tracy は相手の Yumi に伝わるように指示ごとに区切っています。

3-3 Try It Out

Giving Instructions

Affirmative	Negative
Try to …	Try not to …
You need to …	You shouldn't …
Please …	Don't …

Practice using the above expressions of "Giving Instructions."
上記の「指示を出す」表現を使う練習をしましょう。

Student A: Give instructions to your partner on how to do the following Exercises 1 and 2. Fill in the blanks with the expressions above.
下記の Exercise 1 と 2 の空欄に適切な表現を上記から選び、相手に指示を出しましょう。

Student B: Listen to your partner and follow the instructions.
パートナーの指示に従い体を動かしてみましょう。

Example: Deep Breathing

Student A: First, please (place) your hands on your belly and relax your shoulders.
Student B: (Follow the instructions.)
Student A: Next, try to (inhale) slowly to the count of 5 and feel your belly expand. And then, please (breathe) out slowly through your nose to the count of 5.
Student B: (Follow the instruction)
Student A: Try not to (breathe) through your mouth.

Exercise 1: Hand Massage

- First, _____ (shake) your hands gently.
- Next, with your thumb, _____ (massage) one finger on your other hand by going up and down. One finger at a time.
- And then, with your thumb, _____ (make) circles on the heel of the other hand.
- _____ (move) your thumb too fast.

Exercise 2: Tapping Therapy

- First, _____ (tap) your head with all of your fingers, imagining that rain is falling on you.
- Next, _____ (go down) your face, neck, shoulder, arms, belly, legs, onto your toes.
- And then, _____ (imagine) how wet you are. (imagine) the sun coming out and drying you off.
- _____ (open) your eyes yet and feel the warmth of the sun.

Part 4 Outcome

Follow the steps below. Then introduce your favorite stress-relief strategy or things you do when you want to feel happy. Present it with pictures or illustrations.

以下のステップに従ってください。そして、クラスメイトにお勧めできるストレス発散法や、悲しいときに立ち直れる方法紹介してください。写真やイラストを使いながら、以下の手順で話してください。

Step 1: Brainstorming: Think of all the ways you can relieve stress. You can write or draw your ideas in a mind map.

Example: Create a mind map about how you relieve stress and relax.

YOUR MIND MAP

my stress-relief strategies

*You can draw this in your notebook or on a separate piece of paper

Step 2: Organizing your ideas: Using the mind map you created, decide what and how you will tell the story of your stress relief strategy.

Step 3: Telling your story: Tell your story to your partner.

Step 4: Creating visuals: Think of visuals (i.e., actual items, pictures of the items, places, actions) you would like to show when telling your story to your classmates.

Part 5 Reflection

Check your progress. Circle the numbers below.

今回のレッスンを振り返りましょう。下の番号に○を付けましょう。

Now I can ...	☹ ← ---- → ☺
1. talk about the topic of this unit. (Zen and stress relief strategies)	1---2---3---4---5
2. write about myself using the expressions in Part 2.	1---2---3---4---5
3. use the communication tips in Part 3. (giving instructions)	1---2---3---4---5
4. talk about my personal experience/feelings. (stress-relief strategy)	1---2---3---4---5

Unit 14 MY FAVORITE LOCAL DISH

Part 1 Exploring the Topic

1-1 First Impression

A Traditional Dish From My Hometown

Profile

Risa Kurahashi graduated from the San Francisco State University MA TESOL program in 2004. She is currently working as an English program curriculum developer and a teacher trainer with many English native speakers in Tokyo. She is into scuba diving, traveling, and cooking.

Look at the picture and the title. Write your predictions about the story.
写真とタイトルを見てみましょう。ストーリーについて、あなたの予想を書きましょう。

1-2 Listening

15

Key Words

prefecture 県　traditional dish 伝統料理・郷土料理
childhood memories 子ども時代の思い出　recover 回復する　pour 注ぐ
boil 煮る　add 加える　ingredient(s) 材料　catch a cold 風邪をひく
with special memories attached 特別な思い出と共に

Listen to the Opening Story and answer the following questions.
オープニングストーリーを聴いて、以下の質問について答えましょう。

1. What's the traditional dish in Risa's hometown that brings back special memories? Have you ever tried it before?
2. Are there any local dishes from your hometown that bring back special memories to you?

1-3 Opening Story

Read and check the contents of the Opening Story you heard in the Listening Section.
リスニングで聴いた Opening Story の内容を確認しましょう。

A Traditional Dish From My Hometown

My hometown is in Aichi prefecture. Aichi has many interesting traditional dishes. For example, *misokatsu* (pork cutlet with red miso), and *hitsumabushi* (white rice topped with grilled eel). *Miso nikomi udon* is another one. It is thick wheat noodles with red miso soup. Red miso was originally made in Aichi. The noodles are harder than regular noodles, so some people think the noodles are not cooked well.

It is not only a traditional dish in Aichi but also a special dish for me because I have good childhood memories of it. When I was sick, my mother always cooked the noodles with chicken, green onions, and eggs to help me recover. I felt deep love from my mother although she rarely showed how much she loved me. When I eat the noodles, it still warms my heart.

I will tell you how to make *miso nikomi udon*. First, chop green onions and slice *kamaboko* (fish cake). Then, pour some water into a small pot and boil them. Next, add chicken pieces. After that, add noodles. Then add red miso. Finally, add an egg.

I studied abroad in the US and lived with my host family. My host mother made chicken soup for me when I caught a cold. There is a similar culture over there of parents cooking for their children when they are sick. I am sure you have a local dish in your hometown with special memories attached.

1-4 Grammar Tips

Adverbs of Sequence (first, next, after that, finally) are used when you explain something such as how to cook, how to use a machine such as a washing machine, how to wear clothes, how to put on makeup. They are used so that listeners can follow directions or steps of a process or demonstration.

順序を表す first（最初に）, next（次に）, after that（その後）, then（それから）, finally（最後に）などは料理の調理法、洗濯機など機器の使い方、衣服の着方、裁縫の手順、メイクの仕方など出来事の順番をわかりやすく示す時に使います。プレゼンテーションやライティングでもよく使われるので表現の幅も広がり、とても便利です。

Example: How to make *miso nikomi udon* 味噌煮込みうどんの作り方

First, chop green onions and slice *kamaboko* (fish cake). Then, pour some water into a small pot and boil them. Next, add chicken pieces. After that, add noodles. Then, add red miso. Finally, add the rest of the ingredients and an egg.

Part 2 Expressing Yourself

A. Practice writing about yourself in English using some of the expressions below. Use the examples in the parentheses as a reference and change the colored parts into your own words.

下記の表現の型を使って、自分のことを書けるようにしましょう。括弧内の例を参考にして茶色の部分の単語を自分の言葉に置き換えてください。

伝統 / 郷土料理を紹介する表現 : What is a traditional dish from your hometown?

1. It is **red miso**, originally made in <**Aichi**>.
   (the name of traditional dish) (the name of your hometown)

特別な理由を説明する表現 : Why is it special for you?

2. Because I have **good childhood memories** of it.
   (e.g., great memories, warm memories)

思い出について話す表現 : What do you remember about it?

3. When I **was sick**, **my mother** always **cooked** <***miso nikomi udon***>.
(e.g., was a child, went to <place>) (e.g., my dad, my grandmother) (e.g., bought, gave)

B. Write about a traditional dish in your hometown including a reason why it's special to you in English using the sentences/phrases/expressions above.
上記のの文章 / 句 / 表現を参考に自分の出身地の伝統 / 郷土料理について書き、その料理が自分にとって特別である理由を英語で書きましょう。

The name of a traditional dish in your hometown: ______________________________

Why did you choose it? ______________________________

Why does it bring back special memories? ______________________________

____

Part 3 Communication Practice

3-1 Dialogue: Giving Examples

Please take a look at the following dialogue and think about when the underlined expression will be used.
下記の対話を見てみましょう。下線部はどのような時に使われていますか。

Ben: Hi Risa, where is your hometown?

Risa: My hometown is in Aichi prefecture.

Ben: Please tell me about a traditional dish in your hometown.

Risa: Let me see ... There are many interesting local dishes in my hometown. For example, *miso nikomi udon* is one of them.

Ben: What is it?

Risa: It is hot noodles with vegetables and chicken with red miso soup. Red miso was originally made in Aichi.

Ben: It sounds delicious. What kinds of vegetables do you cook?

Risa: Ah, for instance, mushrooms and green onions.

Ben: I see. Is it special or important for you?

Risa: Yes! When I was sick in early childhood, my mother always cooked it. It brings back good memories whenever I eat it.

3-2 Communication Tips: Giving Examples

Adding examples helps you express your ideas and opinions more clearly to others. It also makes others more interested in you and the conversation. Try to use these tips.

具体例を加えることで自分の考えをより明確に相手に伝えることができるだけでなく、相手の興味関心を引くため、会話も弾みます。是非積極的に使いましょう。

3-3 Try It Out

Giving Examples

For example,/For instance,	例えば
One example is ...	１つの例としては…
Another example is ...	別の例としては…

Practice using the above expressions of “Giving Examples.”

上記の「具体例を挙げて答える」表現を使う練習をしましょう。

Student A: Choose a topic from the box below, and say “Please tell me about (the topic you chose).”

下記の四角の中からトピックを選び、“Please tell me about（選んだトピック）” で会話を始めます。

Student B: Give three examples and explain about the chosen topic as much as possible.

そのトピックに関して 3 つの具体例を挙げて説明しましょう。

After finishing, switch the roles of A and B.

その後、A と B の役割を交代しましょう。

Example

Student A: Please tell me about <a traditional/special dish in your hometown>.

Student B: Let me see. There are many interesting traditional dishes in my hometown. For example, miso nikomi udon is one of them.

Topics

1. favorite music **2. favorite food** **3. favorite cafe**
4. favorite movie **5. your idea**

Part 4 Outcome

Follow the steps below. Then introduce the story of a traditional dish from your hometown. Present it with pictures or illustrations.

次のステップに従ってください。そして、自分の出身地の伝統 / 郷土料理を紹介しましょう。写真やイラストを使いながら、以下の手順で紹介してください。

Step 1: Brainstorming: Think about some traditional dishes from your hometown and list them all. After that, choose one dish that brings special memories.

Step 2: Organizing your ideas: Write about the dish, answering the questions below:

1. Where is your hometown?
2. What is the name of a traditional dish in your hometown? What is it? (describe it, what are the ingredients?, how is it cooked?) Name some examples.
3. Why is it special or important for you?
4. How do you make the dish? Use “first,” “then,” “next,” “after that,” “finally.”

Step 3: Creating visuals: Find a photo of the traditional dish from your hometown or draw it.

Step 4: Telling your story: Share the information about the traditional food in a pair or group. When you listen to each speaker, ask at least one question. For example:

-How often do you eat it? When do you eat it?
-What does it taste like?
-Do you have any other traditional dishes in your hometown? What are they?

Part 5 Reflection

Check your progress. Circle the numbers below.

今回のレッスンを振り返りましょう。下の番号に○を付けましょう。

Now I can ...	☹ ← ---- → ☺
1. talk about the topic of this unit. (traditional dish from my hometown)	1---2---3---4---5
2. write about myself using the expressions in Part 2.	1---2---3---4---5
3. use the communication tips in Part 3. (giving examples)	1---2---3---4---5
4. talk about my personal experience/feelings. (introduce a traditional dish from my hometown)	1---2---3---4---5

Unit 15 MY FAVORITE POP CULTURE

Part 1 Exploring the Topic

1-1 First Impression

The Coolest Japanese Pop Culture

Profile

Risa Kurahashi graduated from the San Francisco State University MA TESOL program in 2004. She worked at a language school in San Francisco, CA and met many students from around the world.

Look at the picture and the title. Write your predictions about the story.
写真とタイトルを見てみましょう。ストーリーについて、あなたの予想を書きましょう。

1-2 Listening

16

Key Words

decorated with	装飾された	around the world	世界中で	attractive	魅力的
cool	かっこいい	be interested in	興味がある	currently	現在
realize	理解する、認識する	appreciate	感謝する	be so proud of	誇りに思う

Listen to the Opening Story and answer the following questions.
オープニングストーリーを聴いて、以下の質問について答えましょう。

1. Why does Kevin choose to wear a Hello Kitty costume?
2. Do you think Japanese pop culture is cooler than Korean or American pop culture? Why? Why not?
3. Which Japanese pop culture do you think is the coolest?

1-3 Opening Story

Read and check the contents of the Opening Story you heard in the Listening Section.
リスニングで聴いた Opening Story の内容を確認しましょう。

The Coolest Japanese Pop Culture

This is Kevin, who is wearing a Hello Kitty costume in the photo. He was my coworker at an English language school in the US. He loves Japanese pop culture as well as Japanese traditional culture. He posted this photo on Halloween Day on SNS. He also posted another photo of a toilet decorated with Hello Kitty wallpaper during his travel in San Diego, California. He thinks Hello Kitty is so cute and much cooler than other characters.

Japanese pop culture is popular around the world, in places such as the US, the UK, France, Korea and so on. Anime, manga, J-pop characters, and cosplay seem more attractive and cooler to people overseas. Hello Kitty is one of them. I was really surprised to know how many people were interested in Japanese pop culture when I lived in the US. I am also currently working with a lot of English teachers from different countries. Most of them say Japanese pop culture is the best and the most interesting in the world. That's why they wanted to come to Japan. They know about Japanese culture better than me.

We sometimes don't realize what we have in our own culture, but it is important for us to know and appreciate what we have as well as show interest in other cultures. As a person from Japan, I am so proud of our culture because some people around the world think Japan and Japanese culture is the coolest.

1-4 Grammar Tips

We use a comparative adjective to express how two people or two things are different, and we use a superlative adjective to show how one person or thing is different to all the others of its group.
人やモノについて両者を比べたり、またそのグループの中で一番（最も）～であることを相手に伝える表現があります。形容詞を用いた Comparatives (比較級) と Superlatives (最上級) です。

Example

◆ Compare and express the difference between two people or two things (Comparatives)

1) Hello Kitty is cooler than *Doraemon*. (形容詞＋ er)
2) Anime seems more attractive than American cartoons. (more + 形容詞)
3) The manga version of *One Piece* is better than the movie version. (不規則変化 : better, worse)

◆ Compare and express one person or thing to all the others of its group (Superlatives)

1) People think Japan and Japanese culture is the coolest in the world. (the 形容詞 ＋ est)
2) Japanese pop culture is the most interesting in the world. (the most + 形容詞)
3) Japanese pop culture is the best in the world. (不規則変化 : the best, the worst)

Part 2 Expressing Yourself

A. Practice writing about yourself in English using some of the expressions below. Use the examples in the parentheses as a reference and change the colored parts into your own words.
下記の表現の型を使って、自分のことを書けるようにしましょう。括弧内の例を参考にして茶色の部分の単語を自分の言葉に置き換えてください。

興味のある文化について : What culture do you want to learn more about?
とその理由 : Why?

1. I want to learn more about **Spanish culture** (e.g., my own culture) because **Spanish fashion** (e.g., Kimono) is **the most stylish** (e.g., the most beautiful).

一番～だと思うもの：Which world pop culture is the most interesting to you?

2. I think **Japanese** pop culture is the most interesting.
(e.g., Korean, American, Spanish)

その理由：Why?

3. It's mainly because **anime** seems more attractive than **Marvel comics**.
(e.g., K-Pop music, Flamenco) (e.g., J-Pop music, Hip-Hop)

B. Write about a culture that interests you in English using the sentences/phrases/expressions above.
上記の文章 / 句 / 表現を参考に興味のある文化について英語で文章を作りましょう。

What pop culture do you want to learn more about? ______________________

Why do you want to learn more about it? ______________________

____

Part 3 Communication Practice

3-1 Dialogue: Asking for Opinions and Giving Opinions

Please take a look at the following dialogue and think about when the underlined expression will be used.
下記の対話を見てみましょう。下線部はどのようなときに使われていますか。

Risa: Hi Barry, you said your sister was interested in Japanese pop culture last time. <u>What do you think about</u> Japanese pop culture<u>?</u>

Barry: <u>I think</u> Japanese pop culture is cooler than American pop culture.

Risa: Oh, really? Why?

Barry: <u>In my opinion</u>, it's the coolest because of the cosplay.

Risa: I see. Akihabara and Harajuku are the best places to see a lot of cosplayers. You must go and take some photos.

Barry: Thank you for the information. Why don't we go together when you have free time?

Risa: Sounds good! I will check out some events and send you the links later.

Barry: Oh, great! Thanks!

3-2 Communication Tips: Asking for Opinions and Giving Opinions

In a global society, it is important to have and express one's own opinions. It is also important to be able to give and ask for opinions in a polite manner.
グローバル社会では自分の意見をしっかり持ち、述べることが重要視されます。常に自分の考えを持ち、意見を求められたら丁寧に答え、また同時に相手の意見を尋ねることができるように練習しましょう。

3-3 Try It Out

Asking for Opinions and Giving Opinions

Asking for Opinions	Giving Opinions
What do you think (about …)? What's your opinion?	I think … In my opinion, …

Practice using the above expressions of "Asking for Opinions and Giving Opinions."
上記の「相手の意見を聞く、自分の意見を言う」表現を使う練習をしましょう。

Student A: Choose a topic from the box below, and ask opinions.
下記の四角の中からトピックを選び、それについて意見を聞きます。

Student B: Give your opinions using comparatives or superlatives.
そのトピックに関して比較しながら自分の意見に理由を添えて伝えましょう。

After finishing, switch the roles of A and B.
その後、A と B の役割を交代しましょう。

Example: Topic-Japanese pop culture vs American pop culture

Student A: What do you think about Japanese pop culture and American pop culture?

Student B: I think Japanese pop culture is cooler than American pop culture because anime and manga have cooler characters. What do you think?

Topics

1. **Japanese food vs American food (e.g., healthy, tasty)**
2. **K-pop music vs. J-pop music (e.g., cool, popular)**
3. **fast fashion vs. luxury brand fashion (e.g., good, cheap)**
4. **your idea**

Part 4 Outcome

Follow the steps below to talk about your own pop culture that you already know and want to know more about, and the world pop culture that is the most interesting to you.

以下のステップに従い、既に知っているがもっと学びたいと思う自国の文化と今最も関心のある外国の文化について話しましょう。

Step 1: Brainstorming: Think of the aspect of your own pop culture that you want to learn more about, and the world pop culture you are interested in. Write as many reasons as possible.

Example:

Your Own Pop Culture	*World Pop Culture*
-	-
-	-

Step 2: Organizing your ideas: Decide what information from your list to keep and what information to leave out.

Step 3: Giving your opinion: Give your opinion about your own pop culture that you want to learn more about, and the world pop culture that is interesting to you. Ask your partner what they think about that culture using communication tips.

Step 4: Creating visuals: Do research on your own pop culture and the world pop culture you talked about. Create a KWL poster.

Your Own Pop Culture		
K (What I know)	W (What I want to know)	L (What I have learned)

World Pop Culture		
K (What I know)	W (What I want to know)	L (What I have learned)

Part 5 Reflection

Check your progress. Circle the numbers below.

今回のレッスンを振り返りましょう。下の番号に○を付けましょう。

Now I can ...	← ---- →
1. talk about the topic of this unit. (the coolest J-pop culture)	1---2---3---4---5
2. write about myself using the expressions in Part 2.	1---2---3---4---5
3. use the communication tips in Part 3. (asking for opinions and giving opinions)	1---2---3---4---5
4. talk about my personal experience/feelings. (own culture and world culture)	1---2---3---4---5

Unit 16 MY PART-TIME JOB EXPERIENCES

Part 1 Exploring the Topic

1-1 First Impression

Profile

After graduating from the MATESOL program at SFSU, Kyoko Oda has worked as an English instructor at a college in the US and at a high school in Japan. She also has worked for global companies for 15 years in Japan. Now as an independent English coach and instructor, she helps people in business and college students improve English skills.

Look at the picture and the title. Write your predictions about the story.
写真とタイトルを見てみましょう。ストーリーについて、あなたの予想を書きましょう。

1-2 Listening

17

Key Words

responsibility 責務、業務　serve （飲食物を食卓に）出す　wedding reception 披露宴
funeral 葬儀　several いくつかの　apologize to ~ ～に謝罪する
mess 混乱、汚れ　decision 決断

Listen to the Opening Story and answer the following questions.
オープニングストーリーを聴いて、以下の質問について答えましょう。

1. Did you like Kyoko's story at her part-time work place? Why? or Why not?
2. How did Kyoko feel when she had an unexpected incident at work? Do you have a similar experience?
3. What lessons did Kyoko learn from the experience? Have you learned anything from an unexpected incident?

1-3 Opening Story

Read and check the contents of the Opening Story you heard in the Listening Section.
リスニングで聴いた Opening Story の内容を確認しましょう。

Learning from Experience

During my first year at a university in Tokyo, I worked part-time at an event hall in Hachioji for several months. My responsibility was to serve food and drink to the guests in wedding or funeral receptions. I never felt excited working there. I just did whatever I was told to do, such as serving food and drinks on the table at the right time.

The worst incident occurred when I was serving a table at a funeral reception. There were about fifteen guests dressed in black suits and dresses. They shared one big long table to eat their lunch. Among the guests, there was a middle-aged man who was talking a lot, so he wasn't eating much. I couldn't take away any plates because he hadn't finished any dishes such as the appetizer, salad, fish, meat, or rice. Then it was time to serve the miso soup. I was holding a tray with miso soup bowls on it in one hand and I was trying to place a bowl in front of him with the other hand. Then suddenly his shoulder touched the tray, and he shouted, "Ouch!"

As you can imagine by now, the soup was all over his black suit. The head waiter and I apologized to him. Then I left the room and never returned. I stayed in the kitchen and helped the kitchen workers dry the dishes. I was shocked and scared about the fact that I ruined their formal gathering. I was also scared that my boss and the head waiter would be angry at me, but neither of them scolded me. My boss advised me that I should say something to get the attention of such a guest before serving food. The head waiter apologized to me for giving me too many miso soup bowls at one time. I felt sorry for the head waiter who had to take care of the mess. She was also worried about me.

I have learned from this experience that I should not do just whatever I am told to do without thinking. Sometimes I need to make my own decisions.

1-4 Grammar Tips

◆ neither of +（複数形の名詞・代名詞）「～のどちらでもない」

This expression is used when two things or people are rejected or used in a negative form.
ふたつのモノ・人のうち、どちらともが当てはまらないことを説明する際に使います。

1. Neither of them accused me.（二人とも私を非難しなかった）
2. Neither of the subjects is* interesting.（その教科のどちらとも好きではない）

*Singular forms of the verb follow when the sentence's subject starts with [neither of + plural nouns/pronouns], however, in modern informal speech, some people use plural forms.
[neither of +（複数形の名詞・代名詞）] が文章の主語である場合、それを受ける動詞の形は、単数形です。しかし、くだけた表現では、複数形を使う人も増えています。

◆ either of +（複数形の名詞・代名詞）「～のうちどちらか」

This expression means one or the other of two things or people.
ふたつのモノ・人のうち、どちらかが当てはまる際に使います。

1. Either of the two witnesses is telling a lie.
2. Henry and Mike are in the classroom now. Will either of them help me bring the books to the library?

Part 2 Expressing Yourself

A. Practice writing about yourself in English using some of the expressions below. Use the examples in the parentheses as a reference and change the colored parts into your own words.
下記の表現の型を使って、自分のことを書けるようにしましょう。括弧内の例を参考にして茶色の部分の単語を自分の言葉に置き換えてください。

アルバイトの経験：Have you ever worked part-time before?

1-1. Yes, I've worked at **an event hall**. My job was to **bring food and drink to guests**.
(e.g., a coffee shop, a restaurant) (e.g., take orders, prepare drinks)

1-2. No, I've never worked part-time before.

アルバイトを通して学んだこと：What have you learned through your experience from your part-time job?

2. I learned that I should **speak clearly when I talk to customers**.
(e.g., ask my boss questions when I don't know something, button up my shirt to look neat)

挑戦したいアルバイト：What part-time job would you like to do?

3. I'd like to **work at a department store as a sales advisor**.
(e.g., work at a fancy cafe as a barista, start up as an assistant editor)

アルバイトの経験で学びたいこと：What makes you want to try the above part-time job?

4. I want to learn **how to display fashion merchandise**.
(e.g., how to provide good service for customers, how a website is written and edited)

B. Write about your experiences in English using the Expressions above. If you have experience working part-time, write about the following 1 and 2. If you don't have experience working part-time, write about the following 3 and 4.

Expressions の例文を参考に自分の経験について英語で文章を作りましょう。アルバイトの経験がある人は、下記の 1、2 番について書きましょう。アルバイトの経験がない人は、下記の 3、4 番について書きましょう。

1. Your part-time working experience: ______________________________
2. Things you learned through the experience: ______________________________
____
3. Part-time job you want to try: ______________________________
____
4. Things you want to learn from the part-time job: ______________________________
____

Part 3 Communication Practice

3-1 Dialogue: Making Apologies & Accepting Apologies

Please take a look at Example 1 and 2. Which conversation is better? Why?

2 つの対話を見てみましょう。どちらの例が良い対話ですか。なぜでしょうか？

Example 1

Yuto: Oh no! You spilled the soup on my expensive suit.

Elise: Oops, but you knocked the tray!

Yuto: Don't be so rude. You should apologize!

Elise: Err, ok, so sorry.

Yuto: I need to speak to the manager.

Example 2

Yuto: Oh no! You spilled the soup on my expensive suit.

Elise: Oh! I am so sorry. I will pay for your dry cleaning.

Yuto: It's ok. It was an accident.

Elise: No, I will pay. I feel so bad. I apologize I should have been careful.

Yuto: Don't worry. Accidents happen.

3-2 Communication Tips: Making Apologies & Accepting Apologies

Different regions and cultures have different definitions of apology and different ways of apologizing. The overuse of "sorry" instead of "thank you" can give the wrong impression to the other party. It is necessary for us to find the appropriate way of apologizing for each situation.

地域や文化によって謝罪の定義や仕方も様々です。"thank you" の代わりに "sorry" を多用して相手に誤った印象を与えてしまうこともあります。地域や文化によって、どの程度の謝罪が適切かどうか考える必要があります。

3-3 Try It Out

Making Apologies and Accepting Apologies

Making Apologies	Accepting Apologies
I'm sorry (for …). I apologize (for …). Excuse me (for …).	No problem. That's alright. Don't worry.

Practice using the above expressions of "Making Apologies and Accepting Apologies."
上記の「謝罪する、謝罪を受ける」表現を使う練習をしましょう。

Student A: Add an apology expression to 1-3 below and read the sentences.
下記の１－３の文に謝罪の表現を付け加え、全文を読みます。

Student B: Use an expression of accepting apology and respond to Student A.
謝罪を受ける表現を使い、Studen A にこたえましょう。

After finishing, switch the roles of A and B.
その後、A と B の役割を交代しましょう。

Example: *at work*
Student A: <u>I apologize for</u> not bringing the document. I left it on my desk and forgot to take it when I left my office.
Student B: <u>No problem</u>. You can email it to me later.

1. *at school*
Student A: (Making an apology) being late. My train was delayed again.
Student B: (Accepting an apology).

2. *on the phone*
Student A: (Making an apology). I've lost my voice. I must have caught a cold.
Student B: (Accepting an apology). Take care.

3. *at work*
Student A: (Making an apology). I made a mistake. I should have confirmed with you before making the decision.
Student B: (Accepting an apology).

Part 4 Outcome

Follow the steps below. Then, tell a story about an experience which you learned something from, or about one of the worst experiences you had and how you overcame it.
以下のステップに従ってください。あなたの経験とその経験から学んだことについて、または、最悪の経験をしてそれをどう克服したかについて、ストーリーを伝えましょう。

Step 1: Brainstorming: Think of experiences at work, school, or in your daily life. Pick one experience which you learned something from.

____

Step 2: Organizing your ideas: Answer the following questions:

Where did it happen? ______________________________

When did it happen? ______________________________

What happened? ______________________________

____

What did you learn from the experience? ______________________________

____

Step 3: Telling your story: Tell your story to your partner.

Step 4: Creating visuals: Make a collage based on your story and explain it to your classmates.

Part 5 Reflection

Check your progress. Circle the numbers below.
今回のレッスンを振り返りましょう。下の番号に○を付けましょう。

Now I can ...	☹ ← ---- → ☺
1. talk about the topic of this unit. (part-time job experience)	1---2---3---4---5
2. write about myself using the expressions in Part 2.	1---2---3---4---5
3. use the communication tips in Part 3. (making and accepting apologies)	1---2---3---4---5
4. talk about my personal experience/feelings. (my experience and what I learned from it)	1---2---3---4---5

Unit 17 JOB INTERVIEWS

Part 1 Exploring the Topic

1-1 First Impression

My Job Interview Experience

Profile

Jeremy Schreiner traveled to over twenty countries, and also lived and taught English in Japan for four years. After that, he moved to California, where he got a Master's degree in Business Administration (MBA). Since he loves mountains he chose to live in Seattle, where he worked at the headquarters of Amazon before he got hired by Facebook.

Look at the picture and the title. Write your predictions about the story.
写真とタイトルを見てみましょう。ストーリーについて、あなたの予想を書きましょう。

1-2 Listening

18

Key Words

recruiter 社員を募集する人　screening 選考　on-site 現地での　poorly ひどく、下手に
start all over again 初めからやり直す　in the end 最終的に
lunch buddy session 現役社員がアドバイスをくれる会合でランチタイムに行われる。
redeem oneself 挽回する　when it comes to ~ 〜に関しては

Listen to the Opening Story and answer the following questions.
オープニングストーリーを聴いて、以下の質問について答えましょう。

1. Do you like Jeremy's advice? Why? Why not?
2. If the interviewer asks you a question you don't understand, what would you do?
3. Have you ever failed at something but kept on trying? What happened when you kept trying?

1-3 Opening Story

Read and check the contents of the Opening Story you heard in the Listening Section.
リスニングで聴いた Opening Story の内容を確認しましょう。

My Job Interview Experience

I'm a data engineer. When I was working at Amazon in Seattle, I got an opportunity to get interviewed at Facebook. My job was good, but I wanted to try something more challenging. In total, there were seven interviews. The first one was a phone interview with a recruiter, and the second one was a technical interview on the computer, which was like a test. There were six questions in thirty minutes. I knew what I had to do, but I was pretty nervous. Luckily, I passed the first two screenings.

Once I passed the phone screenings, they invited me to have on-site interviews. For on-site interviews, the first two were technical interviews and the latter two were non-technical interviews. My second technical interview went extremely poorly. The interviewer asked me some questions I didn't understand. So, I spent half of the interview time following-up questions. While I was asking him questions, he became angrier and angrier. I became less and less confident. When I finally started to write the code, I got only three quarters of the way. Moreover, I realized my coding was wrong and I needed to start it all over again. In the end, I never answered his questions. I could tell from his facial expressions that he wasn't very happy. I also didn't feel confident with my interview, so I was going to give up. During my lunch buddy session, the person who was my lunch buddy told me to never give up. She said, “Everybody makes mistakes and you can redeem yourself.” I reminded myself of her words and kept my mind positive. In the afternoon, the rest of the interviews went well and finally I was offered the job.

My advice for you is to keep trying even if you don’t get the job. Don’t take it personally. It could be just bad luck. When it comes to job interviews, there is so much luck involved. It could be that you or the interviewer are having a bad day or you are asked a difficult question in the interview.

1-4 Grammar Tips

When you want to express “gradually (increasingly),” you can use “become/get” with comparative adjectives.

「だんだん（ますます）～」と表現したいときに、“become/get”と形容詞の比較級を使います。

Example

◆ become / get + 比較級 and 比較級

1. He became angrier and angrier. （彼はだんだん怒ってきた）
2. During the interview, I got less and less nervous.
（インタビュー中、だんだん緊張がほぐれてきた）
3. It is getting colder and colder. （(気温が) だんだん寒くなってくる）

Part 2 Expressing Yourself

A. Practice writing about yourself in English using some of the expressions below. Use the examples in the parentheses as a reference and change the colored parts into your own words.
下記の表現の型を使って、自分のことを書けるようにしましょう。括弧内の例を参考にして茶色の部分の単語を自分の言葉に置き換えてください。

落ち込んだ時の表現 : How did you feel when something went wrong?

1. I was **disappointed** with **my bad grade**.
(e.g., discouraged, depressed) (e.g., the results of the test score, the class cancellation)
2. I was frustrated because **I lost the game**.
(e.g., my parents did not understand me, my hard work didn’t pay off)
3. I was **sad**. (e.g., unhappy, blue, down)

励ましの言葉 : What did someone say to encourage you?

4. My **teacher** said to me, “**You can do it**.”
(e.g., coach, mentor) (e.g., Never give up, Hang in there)

5. My **friend** said to me, "**Take it easy**."
(e.g., co-worker, colleague) (e.g., Don't take it personally, Keep trying)

6. My **mother** said to me, "**Believe in yourself**."
(e.g., uncle, senior at college) (e.g., You have another chance, Keep it up)

励ましの言葉を聞いた時に自分が思ったこと : How did you feel when someone gave you encouragement?

7. I felt **happy**. (e.g. encouraged, empowered)

8. I said to myself, "**I can make it**." (e.g., I can do it, I should challenge myself, Never give up)

どんな人にどんな励ましの言葉をかけたいか : Who would you like to encourage? What kind of encouragement would you give?

9. I want to say to my **sister**, "**You are a good pianist**. **Never give up until you win a prize**."
(e.g., brother, cousin, friend) (e.g., Take it easy, Don't take it personally)

B. Write about your experience when you felt sad and someone encouraged you in English using the sentences/phrases/expressions above.
上記の文章 / 句 / 表現を参考に、落ち込んだ時に聞いた励ましの言葉について英語で文章を作りましょう。

What did you say when you felt down? ______________________________

What encouragement did someone give you? ______________________________

____

How did you feel when you were encouraged? ______________________________

____

Part 3 Communication Practice

3-1 Dialogue: Giving Advice

Please take a look at Example 1 and 2. Which conversation is better? Why?
下記の 2 つの対話を見てみましょう。どちらの例が良い対話ですか。なぜでしょうか。

Example 1

Jackson: What's wrong with you? You look sad.

Hana: I have trouble with my boss at work. Whenever I think about it, I feel sick.

Jackson: (Not again ... she's always going on about the same thing.) Well, you should go and see a doctor.

Hana: What? Don't tell me what to do!

Example 2

Jackson: What's wrong with you? You look sad.

Hana: I have an issue with my boss at work. Whenever I think about it, I feel sick.

Jackson: I see. When you think of your boss, you feel sick. You might want to talk to Human Resources about it.

Hana: Maybe. I'll think about it. Thank you.

3-2 Communication Tips: Giving Advice

When you give someone advice, there are expressions you can use. You can be either indirect or direct depending on the situation.
アドバイスをする際、使う英語の表現によって直接的であったり、間接的であったりします。

3-3 Try It Out

Giving Advice

Indirect	**Direct**
You may ... You might want to ... Perhaps you could ...	You want to ... You should ... You have to ...

Practice using the above expressions of "Giving Advice."
上記の「アドバイスをする」表現を使う練習をしましょう。

Student A: Read the sentences from 1-3 below.
下記の１－３の文を読みます。

Student B: Give advice using the expressions above. Use different types of expressions in this practice.
Aが読んだ文ごとにアドバイスをします。なるべく違う種類の表現を使いましょう。

After finishing, switch the roles of A and B.
その後、AとBの役割を交代しましょう。

Example

1. **Student A:** I have a lot of homework to do, but I forgot what the homework is.
   Student B: ____________________
2. **Student A:** I don't think I love my girlfriend/boyfriend any more.
   Student B: ____________________
3. **Student A:** I have a job interview next Wednesday. I am so nervous and I don't think I can get through it ...
   Student B: ____________________

Part 4 Outcome

Follow the steps below. Then introduce a story of an experience in which you were encouraged by someone or something and have accomplished something because of the encouragement.

以下のステップに従ってください。あなたが励まされ、そのおかげで達成したことについて、ストーリーを伝えましょう。

Step 1: Brainstorming: Think of some things you have achieved because someone or something encouraged you. You may have been encouraged by someone's comments or by other things such as art, music, books, and movies.

Step 2: Organizing your ideas: Choose one achievement and answer the following questions.

When did it happen? ______________________________

What did you achieve? ______________________________

Who or what gave you encouragement? ______________________________

If the encouragement was from a person, what comment did you receive?

____

If the encouragement was from something else, what was the message you received?

____

How did you feel when you received the encouragement above?

____

Now write some advice to yourself from the future to encourage yourself now.

____

Step 3: Telling your story: Tell your story to your partner, based on your answers above.

Part 5 Reflection

Check your progress. Circle the numbers below.

今回のレッスンを振り返りましょう。下の番号に○を付けましょう。

Now I can ...	☹ ← ---- → ☺
1. talk about the topic of this unit. (my experience about receiving encouragement)	1---2---3---4---5
2. write about myself using the expressions in Part 2.	1---2---3---4---5
3. use the communication tips in Part 3. (giving advice)	1---2---3---4---5
4. talk about my personal experience/feelings. (my experience receiving encouragement)	1---2---3---4---5

Unit 18 THE FASHION INDUSTRY

Part 1 Exploring the Topic

1-1 First Impression

Finding My Path in the Fashion Industry

Profile

Chiaki is a fashion artist who explores the possibilities of garments. She earned her Ph.D. at Tokyo University of the Arts in 2019 and now works as a fashion designer and costume designer. She lived in London for her studies and in Paris for her internship for Dior Homme. She presented a capsule collection for Paris Fashion Week 2020.

Look at the picture and the title. Write your predictions about the story.
写真とタイトルを見てみましょう。ストーリーについて、あなたの予想を書きましょう。

1-2 Listening

19

Key Words

unprecedented 前例の無い　power plant 発電所　supplies 供給
priority 優先すること　natural disaster 自然災害　emptiness 虚しさ
ethical 倫理的な　globe 地球　principles 原理原則　sustainability 持続可能性

Listen to the Opening Story and answer the following questions.
オープニングストーリーを聴いて、以下の質問について答えましょう。

1. What direction in fashion did Chiaki take after the earthquake?
2. How would you support sustainability in your life?
3. Have you ever changed your thoughts and actions after a big event? If yes, please share your experience.

1-3 Opening Story

Read and check the contents of the Opening Story you heard in the Listening Section.
リスニングで聴いた Opening Story の内容を確認しましょう。

Finding My Path in the Fashion Industry

On March 11th, 2011, when the Great East Japan Earthquake struck, I was about to go out to take back the shoes that I had rented for my photo shoot. The photo shoot for my collection lasted throughout the night and I came back home on the first train. Then I went to bed and woke up in the afternoon on that day. An unprecedented disaster, a very big earthquake and a tsunami had hit the Fukushima Power Plants. The power and water supplies stopped and all the food disappeared from the stores. Days passed and I found that prioritizing fashion was not appropriate when people needed to survive in a natural disaster. Fashion should have been the last thing to worry about. I started feeling a sense of emptiness. On top of that, I felt the gap between us in Tokyo and the people in Fukushima.

The Great East Japan Earthquake made me reconsider what fashion means to me and to people in society. I kept asking myself, “What is fashion?” To me, fashion is not just for fun or looking fancy; rather, I believe it is deeply connected to people and society.

This experience made me see fashion in a different way. Therefore, I applied to work for a unique ethical fashion brand, which had just started in Japan.

Some of my friends in Europe were already in the ethical fashion industry and I thought this would be a new way of thinking for the future of fashion.

Now I am a fashion designer and artist focusing on sustainable and environment-friendly approaches. I always ask myself, "What can a fashion designer do to protect this one and only planet?" Actually, there are many things that we can do. I believe you should buy the clothes you wear for a long time, from fast fashion to haute couture. It can be one of the ways to support sustainability, and you might be ridiculed because of that. However, whatever other people say, don't give in to the pressure, and believe in yourself. You can find your own way to support sustainability and the earth through fashion.

1-4 Grammar Tips

You can express purpose with "to + Base Form Verb."

「〜するために」という目的を表したい時は、"to 不定詞 + 動詞の原形" を用いて表現します。

Example

1. What can a fashion designer do to protect this one and only planet?
   このたった一つの地球を守るために、ファッションデザイナーは何ができるか？

2. She is working hard to realize her dream.
   彼女は自分の夢を実現するために一生懸命働いている。

Part 2 Expressing Yourself

A. Practice writing about yourself in English using some of the expressions below. Use the examples in the parentheses as a reference and change the colored parts into your own words. See Appendix 10.

下記の表現の型を使って、自分のことを書けるようにしましょう。括弧内の例を参考にして茶色の部分の単語を自分の言葉に置き換えてください。Appendix 10 を参考にしてください。

廃棄（ゴミ）を減らす行動についての表現：What can we do to reduce waste?

1. We can **reuse** items **to reduce waste**.
   (e.g., recycle, donate) (e.g., to save the environment, to slow global warming)

環境に優しい行動についての表現：What can we do to protect the earth at school/home?

2. We can **use our own water bottles** at school.
   (e.g., recycle paper, use the stairs)
3. We can **use an air conditioner for a shorter time** at home.
   (e.g., donate clothes, dispose garbage separately)

既に取り組んでいることについての表現：What do you usually do for SDGs?

4. I **bring my own coffee bottle everyday** to **reduce plastic items**.
(e.g., use my own shopping bag, buy items in a second hand store)
(e.g., reduce waste, stop climate change)

これから取り組もうと思うことについての表現：What will you do for SDGs?

5. I will **buy fair priced items** to **stop child labor** in the world.
(e.g., buy clothes of ethical brands, use the same items for a long time) (e.g., reduce waste)

B. Write about what you will do/what you do to protect the earth in English using the sentences/phrases/expressions above.

上記の文章 / 句 / 表現を参考に自分が地球を守るためにこれからできること、既に取り組んでいることについて英語で文章を作りましょう。

What you will do to protect the earth: ____________________________________

____

What you usually do to protect the earth: ________________________________

____

Part 3 Communication Practice

3-1 Dialogue: Making Suggestions

Please take a look at the following dialogue and think about when the underlined expression will be used.

次の対話を見てみましょう。下線部分はどのような時に使われるか考えてみましょう。

Narumi: We hear the news of climate change quite often.

Ken: I heard that the temperature of the earth is getting higher these days. If the temperature goes up, the ecosystem will collapse. What can we do to stop climate change?

Narumi: Let me see. How about reducing waste in daily life? For example, why don't we use our own water bottles and stop buying plastic bottles?

Ken: That's a good idea! If every one of us tried to reduce waste, there would be less garbage to burn. As a result, the emission of CO_2 will decrease.

Narumi: Oh I see, Ken. Now I understand the connection between our daily activities and SDGs. Let's keep thinking about what we can do to protect our earth and change our ways!

3-2 Communication Tips: Making Suggestions

When making a suggestion in a conversation, you can use the different expressions depending on the relationship with the other person, the situation, and the strength of the suggestion. By using appropriate expressions, it will be easier to convey your suggestions to the person you are talking to.

会話の中で提案するときに、相手との関係、場面、提案の強さによって、ふさわしい表現を使用します。適切な表現を用いることで、相手に提案が伝わりやすくなります。

3-3 Try It Out

Making Suggestions

Let's ...	How about -ing …?
Shall we …?	What about -ing to …?
Why don't we …? (friendly)	Would you like to …? (polite)

Practice using the above expressions of "Making Suggestions."

上記の「提案をする」表現を使う練習をしましょう。

Student A: Choose a topic from the box below, and say "Please give me some suggestions about how to (the topic you chose)."

下記の四角の中からトピックを選び、"Please give me some suggestions about how to (選んだトピック)" で会話を始めます。

Student B: Give some possible suggestions on the topic.

そのトピックに関して、考えられる提案をしましょう。

After finishing, switch the roles of A and B.

その後、AとBの役割を交代しましょう。

Example

Student A: Please give me some suggestions about "how to stop child labor."

Student B: Ok. How about stop buying fast fashion?

Topics

1. stop child labor **2. reduce poverty** **3. save endangered animals**
4. reduce plastic waste **5. your idea**

Part 4 Outcome

Follow the steps below. Then introduce your opinions about Responsible Consumption and Production, one of the SDGs. Present it with pictures or illustrations.

以下のステップに従ってください。そして、SDGsの1つである「つくる責任つかう責任」について、あなたの意見を紹介します。写真やイラストを使いながら、以下の手順で紹介してください。

Step 1: Preparation: Discuss the questions with your partner.

1. What responsibilities do you have as a producer in the fashion industry? Why?

2. What are you going to do to take responsibility?

3. What responsibilities do you have as a consumer of clothes? Why?

4. What are you going to do to take responsibility?

Step 2: Organizing your ideas: Write down the producers' responsibilities and actions and the consumers' responsibilities and actions.

As a producer

Responsibilites:

Actions:

As a consumer

Responsibilites:

Actions:

Step 3: Giving your opinions: Give your opinions on the responsibilities of production and consumption in the fashion industry to your partner.

Part 5 Reflection

Check your progress. Circle the numbers below.

今回のレッスンを振り返りましょう。下の番号に〇を付けましょう。

Now I can ...	☹ ← ---- → ☺
1. talk about the topic of this unit. (finding my path in the fashion industry)	1---2---3---4---5
2. write about myself using the expressions in Part 2.	1---2---3---4---5
3. use the communication tips in Part 3. (make suggestions)	1---2---3---4---5
4. talk about my personal experience/feelings. (how I am going to achieve SDGs)	1---2---3---4---5

Appendix 1 for Unit 2 - Pronouns

人称代名詞について

❑ 主格　Nominative Case

人称 Person　数 Number		単数 Singular	複数 Plural
1人称　First Person		I（私）	we（私たち）
2人称　Second Person		you（あなた）	you（あなたたち）
3人称 Third Person	男性 Masculine	he（彼）	they（彼ら）
	女性 Feminine	she（彼女）	
	中性 Neuter	it（それ）	
	ノンバイナリー Nonbinary	they（話題となるその人）	

❑ 所有格　Possessive Case

人称 Person　数 Number		単数 Singular	複数 Plural
1人称　First Person		my（私の）	our（私たちの）
2人称　Second Person		your（あなたの）	your（あなた方の）
3人称 Third Person	男性 Masculine	his（彼の）	their（彼らの）
	女性 Feminine	her（彼女の）	
	中性 Neuter	its（それの）	
	ノンバイナリー Nonbinary	their（話題となるその人の）	

❑ 目的格　Objective Case

人称 Person　数 Number		単数 Singular	複数 Plural
1人称　First Person		me（私を）	us（私たちを）
2人称　Second Person		you（あなたを）	you（あなた方を）
3人称 Third Person	男性 Masculine	him（彼を）	them（彼らを）
	女性 Feminine	her（彼女を）	
	中性 Neuter	it（それを）	
	ノンバイナリー Nonbinary	them（話題となるその人を）	

❑ 所有代名詞　Independent Possesive

人称 Person　数 Number		単数 Singular	複数 Plural
1人称　First Person		mine（私のもの）	ours（私たちのもの）
2人称　Second Person		yours（あなたのもの）	yours（あなた方のもの）
3人称 Third Person	男性 Masculine	his（彼のもの）	theirs（彼らのもの）
	女性 Feminine	hers（彼女のもの）	
	中性 Neuter	its（それのもの）	
	ノンバイナリー Nonbinary	theirs（話題となるその人のもの）	

❑ 再帰代名詞　Reflexive Pronoun

人称 Person　数 Number		単数 Singular	複数 Plural
1人称　First Person		myself（私自身）	ourselves（我々自身）
2人称　Second Person		yourself（あなた自身）	yourselves（あなたがた自身）
3人称 Third Person	男性 Masculine	himself（彼自身）	themselves（彼ら自身）
	女性 Feminine	herself（彼女自身）	
	中性 Neuter	itself（それ自身）	
	ノンバイナリー Nonbinary	themself（話題となるその人自身）	

Watanuki et al., 2000 を元に作成

⁂ Neutral pronouns refer to organisms, objects, and matters for which gender cannot be determined. Examples include a newborn, a fish, a chair and a meeting for which gender cannot be distinguished.

e.g.,) What a beautiful baby! Is it a boy?

⁂ Nonbinary third person singular is used as a new usage of the existing language "they" by those who do not wish to express gender in the traditional female or male of she/her/her/herself or he/his/him/himself. The verb takes the plural form.

e.g.,) Andy said that they wanted to be open about their new identity,
but they weren't ready to speak about it.

中性代名詞は、男女の判断のつかない生物・物・事物を指します。例えば、男女の判；別ができない新生児、魚、椅子、会議などです。

e.g.,) What a beautiful baby! Is it a boy?

ノンバイナリーを表す 3 人称単数は、she/her/her/herself や he/his/him/himself の従来の女性または男性でジェンダーを表したくない人々が、既存の言語 they を新しい用法として使用する 3 人称単数です。動詞は複数形を取ります。

e.g.,) Andy said that they wanted to be open about their new identity,
but they weren't ready to speak about it.

Example Dialogue of Self-introduction with Gender Pronouns

Jack : Hi, Nana. How's it going? Let me introduce my classmate. This is Alex.
Nana : Hi, Alex. I'm Nana. My pronouns are she and her. Nice to meet you.
Alex : Hi, Nana, nice to meet you. My pronouns are they/them.
<A few days later>
Nana : John, where is Alex? I want to ask him about a new assignment.
Jack : Actually, Alex uses they/them pronouns.
Nana : Oh, that's right. Thanks. Where are they? I want to talk with them.

A new style of communication using personal pronouns (gender pronouns) such as she/her, he/him, and they/them has started spreading.Examples can be found in dance classes, school classes, online meetings, and other opportunities to introduce oneself using gender pronouns.By including preferred gender pronouns in communication, individuals have the right and freedom to choose gender pronouns that they would like to use, which shows their gender identities.

Everyone makes mistakes. When you make a mistake with a pronoun, don't worry. Just apologize, repeat using the correct pronoun, and continue the conversation. With practice and repetition, even unfamiliar expressions will come naturally. As the dialogue above shows, even if the person whose pronoun is mistaken is not present, pointing out the mistake models to others that a correction can be done in a friendly way. This is important for respecting and including transgender and nonbinary people. Everyone wants to be accepted and treated equally. Using "they" as a nonbinary singular gender pronoun can ensure all people are included.

新しいコミュニケーションスタイルとして、she/her、he/him、they/them などの各々が選択した人称代名詞（ジェンダープロナウン）を使うことが広がり始めています。例としては、ダンス教室・学校の授業・オンライン会議の中などでジェンダープロナウンを使った自己紹介をする機会が見られます。コミュニケーションの中にこれらを含めることで、個人が代名詞を自由に選ぶことができ、自分のジェンダーアイデンティティを示すことができるのです。

誰にでも間違いはあります。代名詞を間違えた時は、すぐに謝り、正しい代名詞を使って会話を進めると良いでしょう。使い慣れない表現も、練習し、繰り返し使うことによって自然と使えるようになります。上記の例のように、誰かが第三者の代名詞を間違えて使っているのを聞いた時にも、丁寧に指摘すると良いでしょう。本人がその場にいなくても、使うべき代名詞を間違えた場合は、それを指摘することで、フレンドリーな方法で訂正ができることを他の人に示すことができます。このことは、トランスジェンダーやノンバイナリーの人々を尊重し、受け入れるために重要です。誰もが、受け入れられて平等に扱われることを望んでいます。ノンバイナリー三人称単数形人称代名詞「彼ら (they) 」を使うことで、すべての人を含むことができます。

参考 : Harvard University, University of Washington 各公式サイト

Appendix 2 for Unit 4 - Colors / *Colours (*British English)

off white オフホワイト	vivid orange 鮮やかな橙色	deep green 深緑
ivory アイボリー	crimson 深紅	navy blue 紺
beige ベージュ	magenta マゼンタ	sky blue スカイブルー
pale pink 薄いピンク	khaki カーキ	charcoal gray *grey 炭黒
orange オレンジ	bright yellow 明るい黄色	jet black 漆黒

Appendix 3 for Unit 4 - Fashion Items

Basic fashion items (*British English)

Tops

1. T-shirt

2. sleeveless top

3. sweater vest/ *knitted tank top

4. camisole

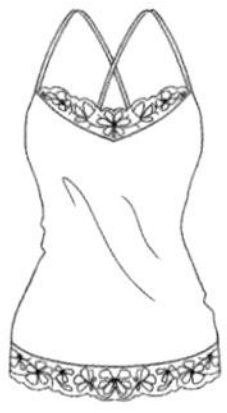

5. blouse

6. long-sleeved shirt

7. short-sleeved shirt

8. hoodie

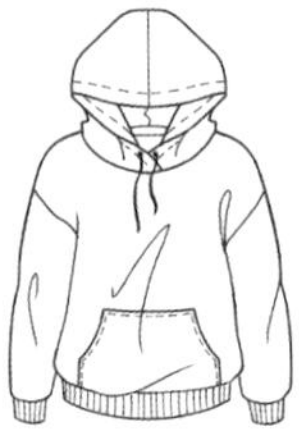

9. sweater/ *jumper

10. cardigan

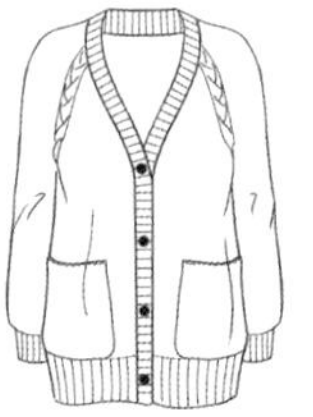

1. T シャツ　2. ノースリーブトップス　3. ニットベスト　4. キャミソール　5. ブラウス
6. 長袖シャツ　7. 半袖シャツ　8. パーカー　9. セーター　10. カーディガン

Bottoms

11. jeans

12. pants/ *trousers

13. skirt

14. shorts

15. culottes

11. ジーンズパンツ　12. ズボン、パンツ　13. スカート
14. 半ズボン、ショートパンツ　15. キュロットスカート

Outerwear

16. coat

17. leather jacket

18. blazer/jacket

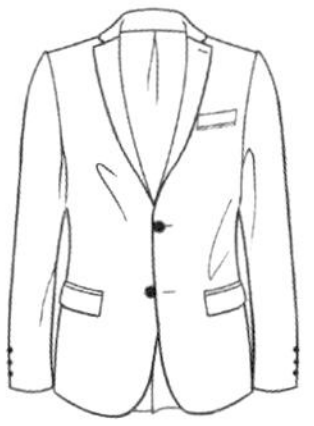

19. down/puffer jacket

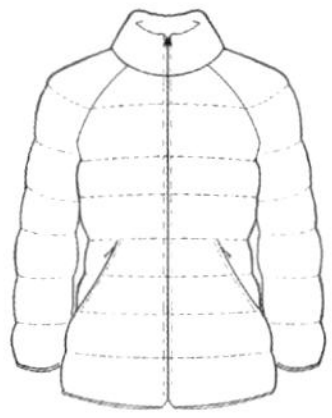

20. gilet

16. コート　17. 革ジャン　18. ブレザー、背広　19. ダウンジャケット　20. ジレ（袖なしの胴着）

Dresses/One-piece outfit

21. dress

22. gown

23. jumpsuit

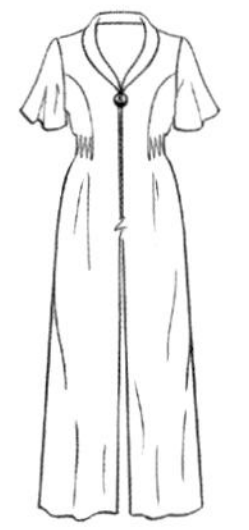

24. overalls

21. ドレス／ワンピース　22. ガウン（パーティーなどの正装に着る）
23. ジャンプスーツ（落下傘降下服に似た上下つなぎの服）　24. オーバーオール、つなぎ服

Sports/Athleisure wear

25. sports bra

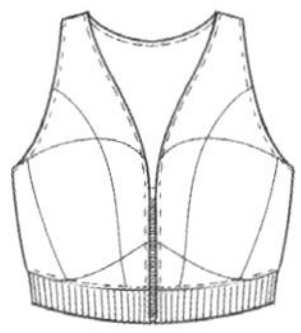

26. sweatshirt

27. sweatpants

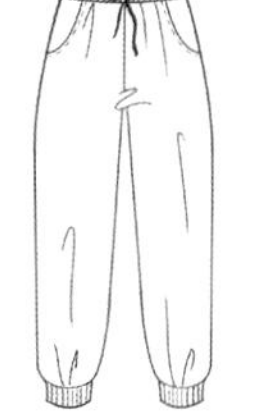

28. running pants

29. yoga pants

25. スポーツブラ（スポブラ）　26. スウェットシャツ、トレーナー
27. スウェットパンツ、トレーニングパンツ　28. ランニングパンツ　29. ヨガパンツ

Footwear

30. high top sneakers/high tops/*trainers

31. running shoes

32. loafers

33. boots

34. sandals

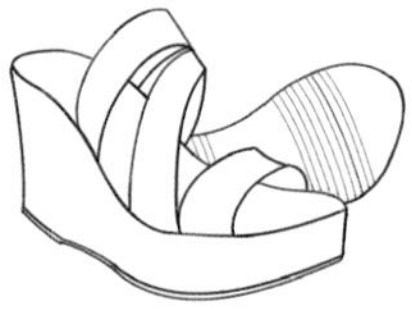

35. flip flops/beach sandals

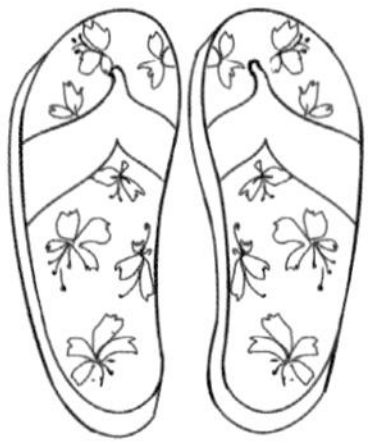

36. pumps

37. dress shoes

38. mules

39. rain boots/rubber boots/*wellington boots (wellies)

30. ハイカットスニーカー　31. ランニングシューズ　32. ローファー　33. ブーツ 34. サンダル
35. ビーチサンダル　36. パンプス　37. ドレスシューズ　38. ミュール　39. 雨靴 / ゴム長靴

Accessories

40. beret

41. scarf

42. earrings

43. purse/shoulder bag/crossover bag

44. backpack /*rucksack

40. ベレー帽　41. スカーフ　42. イヤリング（ピアスも含む）
43. ショルダーバッグ / ハンドバッグ　44. バックパック / リュックサック

Appendix 4 for Unit 4 - Clothing Size Charts

❑ Women's clothing sizes

Japan	5	7	9	11	13	15
US	2	4	6	8	10	12
UK/Australia	6	8	10	12	14	16
EU/France	34	36	38	40	42	44
Italy	38	40	42	44	46	48

✻ Sizing also varies from brand to brand. The sizing applies to outerwear, dresses, pants, skirts and tops.
サイズはブランドにより異なります。アウター、ドレス（ワンピース）、ズボン、スカート、トップスにそれぞれサイズがあります。

❑ Men's clothing sizes (suits, jackets, coats)

Japan	32	34	36	38	40	42
US	30	32	34	36	38	40
UK/AUS	30	32	34	36	38	40
EU	40	42	44	46	48	50

✻ Sizing varies from brand to brand. In Europe, countries, such as France, Germany, Italy, Spain, Sweden, Netherlands, and Portugal, have their own variations.
サイズはブランドにより異なります。欧州では、フランス、ドイツ、イタリア、スペイン、スウェーデン、オランダ、ポルトガルなどでサイズが異なります。

❑ Men's shirt sizes (collars)

Japan/EU (cm)	36	37	38	39	40	41
US/UK (inches)	14	14.5	15	15.5	16	16.5

❑ Men's pants sizes (trousers)

Japan	32	34-36	38-40	42-44	46-48
US	30 (S)	32-34 (M)	36-38 (L)	40-42 (XL)	44-46 (XXL)
UK	30	32-34	36-38	40-42	44-46
EU	46	48-50	52-54	58-60	62-64

✻ Sizing varies from brand to brand.
サイズはブランドにより異なります。

Appendix 5 for Unit 5 - Patterns and Prints

plain
無地

floral
花柄プリント

polka dot
ポルカドット / 水玉模様

(diagonal) stripe
(斜め) ストライプ

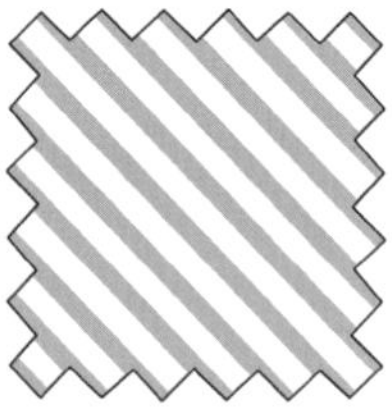

(vertical) stripe
(縦) 縞模様

(horizontal) stipe
(横) 縞模様 / ボーダー

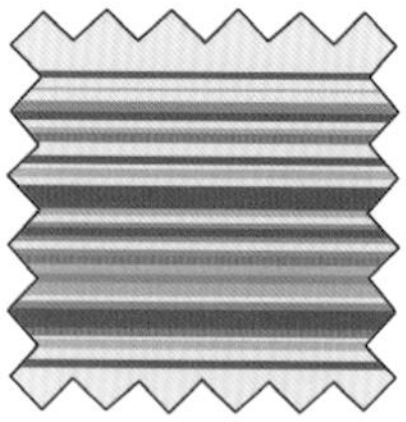

plaid/*tartan
チェック / 格子柄

gingham/*gingham check
ギンガムチェック

abstract
抽象柄

camouflage
カモフラージュ

animal print (leopard print)
ヒョウ柄

animal print (zebra print)
ゼブラ柄

✻ “Border” is used only in Japanese. It is “stripe” or a “striped” shirt as in a phrase.
日本語では「ボーダー」と呼ばれますが、英語では stripe または、句の中で a striped shirt のように表現します。

Choosing and describing clothes for a vacation.

The travel destination 行き先（国、都市）

Fashion items you want to take ＊ Include details such as color, pattern, and material. 色、柄、素材などの詳細も書きましょう。	Why? なぜそのアイテムを持っていくのか理由も書きましょう。
1.	
2.	
3.	
4.	
5.	

Appendix 6 for Unit 5 - Describing Fabrics and Materials

❑ **Exercise:**

Fill in the boxes with items that you find in your daily life.
以下の空欄に当てはまる身の回りのアイテムを書き入れましょう。

Fabric/Material	Items
leather	a jacket, a belt, boots,
straw	
fur	
rubber	
metal	
glass	
plastic (PVC)	
silk	
polyester	
linen	
wool	
nylon	
faux/fake fur	

Practice explaining the items you listed above.
上記のアイテムを説明してみましょう。

Examples:

I have (a/an) ________________ ________________.
〈material〉 〈item〉

I have ________________ ________________.
〈material〉 〈item〉

Appendix 7 for Unit 6 - Fashion Trends

Eras	1920s	1950s	1960s
The look			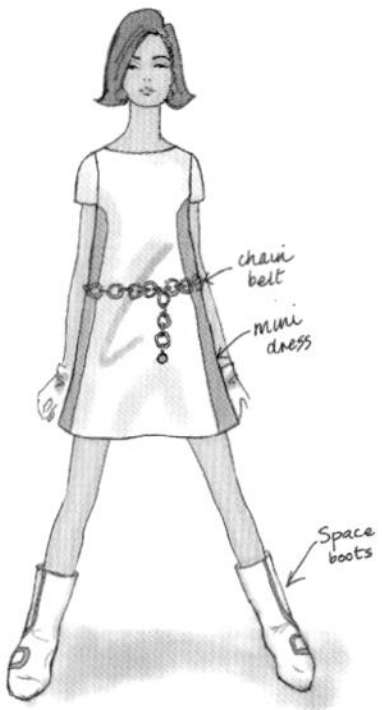
Items	Flapper Dress, Shift Dress (Chanel's Little black Dress), Vionett's Bias-cut evening dress, Chanel suit, pleated skirt, wrap overcoat, fur coat, Cloche hat, stockings.	Circle skirt, Poodle skirt, Pencil skirt, Capri pants, peddle pushers, jeans, sweater, sheath dress, cocktail dress, Bobby socks, beaded cardigan, twinset.	Mini skirt, Mini dress, Maxi dress, knee-length boots, mid-calf boots, space boots, chain belt.
Designers	Coco Chanel Madeleine Vionnet Elsa Schiaparelli Jean Patou Norman Hartnell	Christian Dior Christóbel Balenciaga Charles James Pierre Balmain Jaques Fath	Mary Quant André Courrèges Pierre Cardin Emilio Pucci Jean Muir Paco Rabanne
Styles, trends and silhouettes	Dropped waistline and short hemlines Bobbed haircut (Trend names) La Garconne The Flapper Girl Boyish	Feminine silhouette (small waist, full skirt) Teenage pop culture	Op Art - polka dot prints Hippie trend Short to long hemlines A-line
Inspiration and influences	★ The Roaring Twenties ★ Art Art Deco, Surrealism, Modernism and Feminism. ★ Jazz music Charleston dance "Flapper Girl" craze ★ Hollywood ★ Women's liberation	★ New Look by Christian Dior ★ Movies ★ Music ★ Pop culture	★ Swinging Sixties ★ "Space Age" fashion ★ Jackie Kennedy ★ Musicians The Beatles, Janis Joplin, Jimi Hendrix ("Hippie" look). ★ Pop art

Appendix 8 for Unit 7 - Fashion Styles (Items and occasions)

In this section, you will practice how to describe a fashion style. As you can see in the table below, you can describe a fashion style by describing its clothing items and by saying what situation or occasion it should be worn in or at.

ここではファッションスタイルを説明する表現を練習しましょう。下の表にあるようにそのファッションの特徴的なアイテムや、色などを説明したり、どのようなシチュエーションに着るべきかを伝えることで説明できます。

Fashion Style	Items and Occasions
formal 	**Men's:** suit, shirt & tie, bow tie, morning suit, vest (*waistcoat). **Women's:** cocktail dress, evening dress, formal gown, suit, kimono（振袖／訪問着） **Unisex:** blazer **Occasion:** wedding, formal party, classical concert, VIP event, the opera.
business formal 	**Men's:** dark suit, dress shirt, tie. **Women's:** overcoat, blazer jacket, business suit (skirt & pants), dress. **Unisex:** business suit **Occasion:** job interview, business presentation, business meeting, business lunch or dinner.
business casual 	**Men's:** collared shirt, polo shirt, chinos, cardigan. **Women's:** casual jacket, casual dress, designer jeans, sweater (*jumper), shirt, ablouse. **Occasion:** work, business lunch or dinner.

Fashion Style	Items and Occasions
casual 	**Unisex:** jeans, polo shirt, T-shirt, denim jacket, jeans, checked shirt, casual pants, cargo pants, hoodies, shorts. **Occasion:** at home, hanging out with friends, shopping, traveling, concert, event, night out.
sportswear/athleisure 	**Unisex:** tracksuit, sweat pants, sneakers, T-shirt, sweatshirt, tank top, leggings. **Occasion:** at home, hanging out with friends, shopping, traveling, exercising.
streetwear 	**Unisex:** wide-flared pants, oversized top, ripped-up T-shirt, customized leather jacket, denim jacket, damaged jeans, army pants, bright athletic wear, sneakers, boots. **Occasion:** at home, hanging out with friends, a concert, clubbing, shopping, event, music festival.

Appendix 9 for Unit 12 - Map

Practice using the expressions of “Prepositions of Locations.” You can use the map below or your own school site.

「位置関係を示す前置詞」の表現を使う練習をしましょう。下記の地図、または自分の学校について説明しましょう。

Prepositions of Locations

It is on the first/ second/third floor.	1，2，3 階にある	It is close to A.	A の近くにある
It is in front of A.	A の前にある	It is across from A.	A の向かいにある
It is next to A.	A の隣にある	It is on the left/right.	左 / 右側にある
It is behind A.	A の後ろにある		

Example

Student A: (Do you know/Can you tell me/Could you tell me) where the gym is?

Student B: Yes, it’s over there next to Parking A.

Places

1. gym **2. library** **3. cafeteria** **4. admission office** **5. your idea**

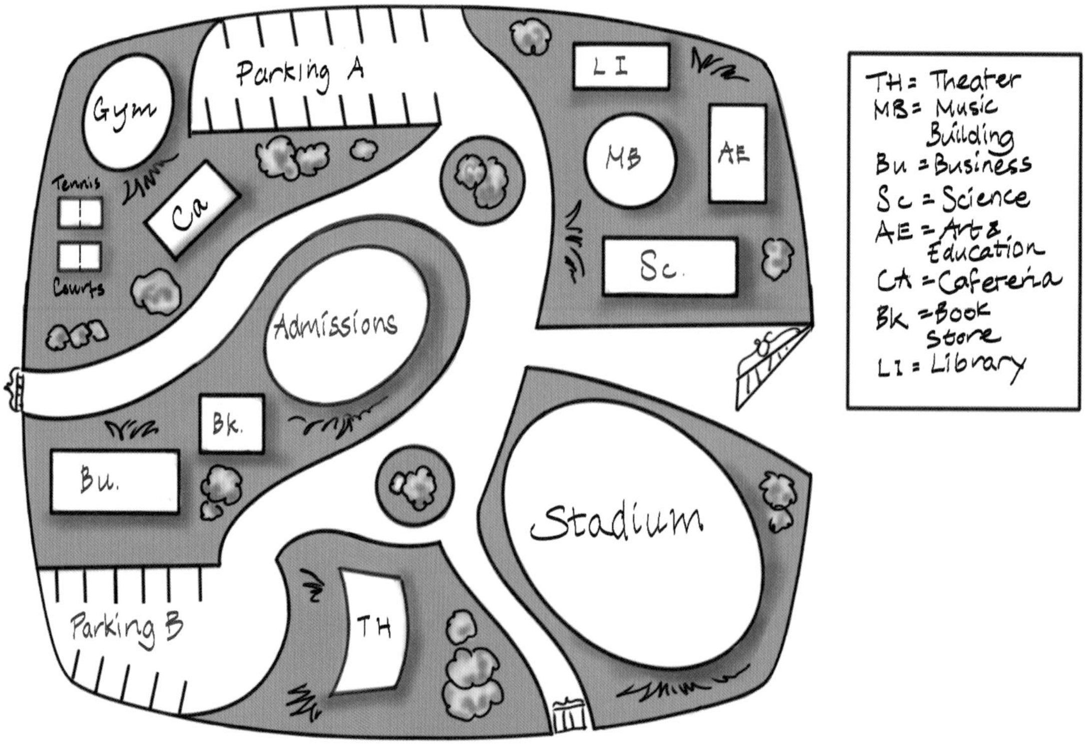

Appendix 10 for Unit 18 - Sustainable Development Goals (SDGs)

Sustainable Development Goals (SDGs) were adopted by the Member States of the United Nations in 2015. The following development goals are excerpts from the 17 development goals to be achieved by 2030.

国連加盟国は 2015 年に持続可能な開発目標 (SDGs) を採択しました。2030 年までに達成を目指している 17 つの目標からの抜粋です。

Goal 1	NO POVERTY 貧困をなくそう	Goal 3	GOOD HEALTH AND WELL-BEING すべての人に 健康と福祉を
Goal 4	QUALITY EDUCATION 質の高い教育を みんなに	Goal 7	AFFORDABLE AND CLEAN ENERGY エネルギーをみんなに そしてクリーンに
Goal 8	DECENT WORK AND ECONOMIC GROWTH 働きがいも 経済成長も	Goal 10	REDUCED INEQUALITY 人や国の不平等 をなくそう
Goal 12	RESPONSIBLE CONSUMPTION AND PRODUCTION つくる責任 つかう責任	Goal 13	CLIMATE ACTION 気候変動に 具体的な対策を
Goal 14	LIFE BELOW WATER 海の豊かさを守ろう	Goal 15	LIFE ON LAND 陸の豊かさも 守ろう

Source: the United Nations Sustainable Development Goals website

出典：国連 持続可能な開発目標ウェブサイト https://www.un.org/sustainabledevelopment/

The content of this publication has not been approved by the United Nations and does not reflect the views of the United Nations or its officials or Member States.

編著者

小塚暁絵　川守田恭枝　コリンズ・キム 園子

著　者

伊藤怜子　宇治田成美　小田恭子　倉橋理佐　坂本優美子　武藤牧子

Forward Mode: English for Fashion Students

ファッションを学ぶ人のための英語コミュニケーション　[B-954]

1　刷　2022年10月4日

編著者　小塚 暁絵　Akie Nyui-Kozuka
川守田 恭枝　Yasue Kawamorita
コリンズ・キム 園子　Kim S. Collins

発行者　南雲　一範　Kazunori Nagumo
発行所　株式会社　南雲堂
〒162-0801　東京都新宿区山吹町361
NAN'UN-DO Co., Ltd.
361 Yamabuki-cho, Shinjuku-ku, Tokyo 162-0801, Japan
振替口座 : 00160-0-46863
TEL:　03-3268-2311（営業部：学校関係）
03-3268-2384（営業部：書店関係）
03-3268-2387（編集部）
FAX:　03-3269-2486
編集者　加藤　敦

組　版　スタジオA. Kato

装　丁　銀　月　堂

検　印　省　　略

コード　ISBN978-4-523-17954-2　C0082

Printed in Japan

E-mail : nanundo@post.email.ne.jp
URL : https://www.nanun-do.co.jp/